Corel

PaintShop Pro 2023

A Comprehensive Guide to Expert Techniques, Tips, and Tricks for Perfecting Your Digital Artistry and Photo Editing Skills

Alexander Grant

TABLE OF CONTENTS

INTRODUCING COREL PAINTSHOP PRO 2023

Welcome to the world of Corel PaintShop Pro 2023 – your gateway to unleashing your creativity, enhancing your photos, and mastering the art of digital imaging. Whether you're a seasoned professional, an aspiring artist, or a hobbyist looking to elevate your skills, this comprehensive guide is designed to be your ultimate companion on your journey through the powerful features and functionalities of PaintShop Pro 2023.

In this book, we will embark on an exciting exploration of Corel PaintShop Pro, delving deep into its innovative tools, intuitive workflows, and advanced techniques. From basic photo enhancements to complex digital artwork creation, you'll learn how to harness the full potential of this versatile software to bring your creative vision to life.

Chapter by chapter, we'll cover everything you need to know to become proficient in PaintShop Pro 2023. We'll start by familiarizing ourselves with the interface and essential tools, ensuring you have a solid foundation to build upon. As we progress, we'll dive into topics such as photo editing techniques, retouching and restoration, graphic design principles, and much more.

Throughout this journey, you'll discover insider tips, expert tricks, and practical insights to streamline your workflow and achieve professional-quality results. Whether you're editing portraits, landscapes, or creating digital illustrations, you'll find invaluable guidance to elevate your work to the next level.

But this book isn't just about technical instruction – it's also about sparking your imagination and fueling your passion for digital artistry. Alongside step-by-step tutorials and hands-on exercises, you'll find inspiration from real-world examples and creative projects that demonstrate the endless possibilities PaintShop Pro 2023 offers.

Whether you're looking to enhance your personal photos, create stunning graphics for your business, or pursue a career in digital design, Corel PaintShop Pro 2023 is your ultimate tool for turning your ideas into reality. And with this comprehensive guide by your side, you'll be well-equipped to conquer any creative challenge that comes your way.

So, let's embark on this journey together, as we unlock the full potential of Corel PaintShop Pro 2023 and unleash the artist within. Get ready to transform your imagination into breathtaking visuals – the possibilities are limitless!

CHAPTER 1
OVERVIEW OF COREL PAINTSHOP PRO 2023

Introduction

Corel PaintShop Pro is a powerful and flexible piece of software for changing photos and making graphics. PaintShop Pro, which was made by Corel Corporation, has a lot of tools and features that make it useful for both new and experienced users. This is why shooters, artists, and designers all over the world choose it. PaintShop Pro has all the tools you need to make your artistic idea come to life, whether you want to improve your photos, make beautiful digital art, or make eye-catching drawings for different projects. PaintShop Pro can be used for a lot of different kinds of editing, from simple jobs like cutting and color correction to more complex ones like layer-based editing and content-aware tools. The easy-to-use design of PaintShop Pro is one of its best features. It lets users quickly switch between tools and features without getting confused. You can easily change how panels and tools are organized in the area to suit your needs. This will help you get more done and improve your workflow.

PaintShop Pro has a huge library of brushes, patterns, colors, and effects that can be used to try out different artistic ideas. The software has everything you need, whether you're a digital artist who wants to make detailed drawings or a shooter who wants to add an artistic touch to your pictures. PaintShop Pro also has more advanced features, like the ability to edit RAW photos, create HDR images, do batch processing, and use advanced selection tools. These features give you more control and freedom over your projects. Because it can edit images without destroying them, you can try out different effects and changes without changing the original. This keeps your creative process open and changeable. PaintShop Pro has a lot of useful features, and it also has a lot of learning materials, like lessons, tips, and online groups where people can share what they know. PaintShop Pro has everything you need to achieve, whether you're a beginner who wants to learn the basics or an expert user who wants to improve your skills.

Features

- Image editing and graphic design application.
- Supports editing various image details.
- Professional-grade RAW image editing.
- Manage and edit photos easily.
- Adjust photos and layouts for painting effects.
- Offers new maps and smoother performance.
- Features new essentials and complete workspaces.
- Eye-catching models and enhancements.
- Easy working environment with faster performance.
- New creative brush support with rich textures.
- Introduces a new user interface with more customization.
- Includes many other unique features.

System Requirements

- Windows® 11, Windows® 10 (version 1903 or later recommended with latest service pack, 64-bit version).
- For virtualization: Microsoft Windows Server 2012 R2, Windows Server 2016, Windows Server 2019.
- Intel® Celeron G Series or AMD® Phenom II or later (Intel® i5 Series or AMD® Ryzen or later recommended for AI support).
- 4GB RAM (8GB recommended for AI support).
- Requires 3GB of available hard disk space (4GB recommended).
- Screen resolution 1366 x 768 (1920 x 1080 @ 100 DPI recommended). Supports up to 250 DPI with appropriate resolution.
- DirectX 11 or higher compatible video adapter with the latest drivers (DirectX 12 compatible discrete VGA card recommended for GPU acceleration).

Installation and Setup

- **Download**: You can get this file from the official Corel website or an approved dealer. Make sure you download the software that works with your Windows or macOS operating system.
- **Run the installer**: Once the download is done, find the file you got and double-click it to start the setup. This will start the process of installation.

- **Accept the Terms**: The End User License Agreement (EULA) will be shown to you during the download process. It's important to read the deal carefully, and if you agree with the terms, you should accept them.
- **Pick an Installation Method**: After that, you might be asked to pick an installation method. This could mean picking the area where the software will be put and choosing whether to make shortcuts on the desktop or in the Start menu.
- **Wait for the installation to start**. Once you've picked an installation method, click "**Install**" to start the process. Depending on how fast your computer is and what version of PaintShop Pro you're downloading, the process could take a few minutes to finish.
- **Activation**: You may be asked to activate the program after the download is finished. People who bought PaintShop Pro licenses need to enter the serial number or product key that came with their purchase to make the software work. To finish the registration process, follow the steps shown on the screen.
- **Updates**: Once PaintShop Pro is activated, it's a good idea to see if there are any changes available. Bugs may be fixed, speed may be improved, and new features may be added in updates. Most software lets you check for updates right from within it; just go to the Help menu and choose "**Check for Updates**."
- **Launch**: After the download and registration are done, you can start Corel PaintShop Pro from the Apps folder on macOS, the Start menu in Windows, or the desktop link.

CHAPTER 2

INTERFACE AND WORKSPACE

Introduction to the PaintShop Pro Interface

PaintShop Pro has three different areas: *Photography, Essentials, and Complete*. Each one is designed to meet a specific need.

- The **Complete** area gives users access to all of the tools, so it's the default choice for people who want a lot of features.
- The **Essentials** area has a limited set of tools that are meant to be easy to use and see. It's perfect for people who like clean and simple interfaces.
- For editing pictures with a touch screen, the **Photography** area has simple editing tools that make it easy for people who work with pictures.

In addition to the basic choices, users can choose a specific workspace or make and save their workplace that fits their particular working needs.

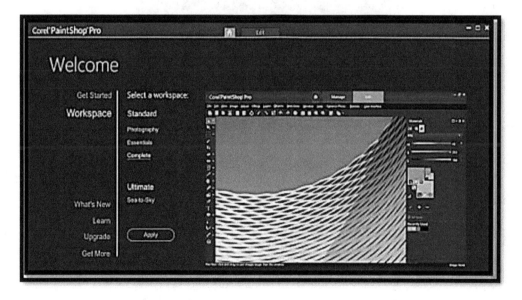

Workspace Layout and Navigation

- **Welcome**: Available in Photography, Essentials, and Complete editions.
- **Manage**: Included in the complete edition.
- **Edit**: Accessible in Photography, Essentials, and Complete editions but is tailored to the editing preferences of each workspace
- **Adjust (optional)**: Available in the **Complete edition** but not as a default tab.

You can access tools and controls through each tab to efficiently complete tasks. Store your current workspace configuration and state, including open pictures, magnifications, screen positions, palettes, toolbars, dialog boxes, and windows, in specific workspaces like Complete.

The Welcome Area

There are learning tools, deals, and important information about your goods on the Welcome page. It also lets you get to the workspace's basic settings, start a new project, or open a file you just saved.

The Manage tab

Through the Manage button in the complete area, you can get to picture management tools that will help you preview, organize, and speed up the photo-editing process.

The things that make up the manage tab:

- **Navigation palette**: Assists in organizing and locating photographs. You can view folders on your computer by using the search box, selecting the Collections or Computer tabs, or sorting photos by collection, tags, or ratings.
- **Preview section**: Offers two views - a large single-image view and a thumbnail view (expanded Organizer palette).

- **Info palette**: Provides details about the selected picture, including exposure settings displayed in a camera-style format. It also includes tabs for adding details like tags and ratings and accessing EXIF or IPTC data.
- **Organizer toolbar**: Offers various options and instructions for managing images. Tools can be shown or hidden by clicking the button.

Edit tab

If you click the Edit tab, you can get to the editing tools. Depending on the location, you can use the options, tools, and panels to make and change pictures.

The following choices are in Edit:

- **Menu bar**: Displays instructions for executing actions. For example, the Effects menu contains controls for applying effects to photographs.
- **Toolbars**: Provide buttons for commonly used commands.
- **Palettes**: Assist in selecting tools, adjusting settings, managing layers, choosing colors, and performing other editing operations by presenting picture data.
- **Image window**: Shows open files, with options for window view or tabbed view.
- **Status bar**: Displays information such as image size, color depth, and pointer location, along with details about the currently selected tool or menu function. The status bar, located at the bottom of the window, remains fixed and cannot be modified or relocated like other toolbars.

Customizing Toolbars, Palettes, and Panels

Some tools in the camera area only need one click, while others have options that you can change. If there are any, the options for the tool you've chosen show up at the bottom of the window. Click Cancel (the x sign) or Apply (the check mark icon) when you are done making changes. Like in other places of work, you can make changes over and over again. Up and Down are on the left side of the Tools panel.

AI features in the Photography workspace

In the photography workplace, there are different AI (artificial intelligence) tools that can be used. It takes some time to look at these traits. How fast things go depends on both the picture size and the speed of your computer. A blue moving layer will be shown while the AI looks at your picture. Use the Esc key to stop processes at any time. For AI Style Transfer to work, the Instant Effects panel is needed. When you click AI Style Transfer and choose the AI-Powered group, the Instant Effects menu opens if it isn't already there. When you click on a style thumbnail the first time, it changes the image. When you click on it twice, it changes your picture. You can't stack styles; when you use a new one, the old one is thrown away.

Decide on your workspace color

There are a range of colors for workspaces, from dark to light. You can also pick a background color for the picture and viewing boxes.

To pick a color for your workspace:

1. Go to View and choose Workspace Color.
2. Pick a color from these options:
   - Gray-Black (default)
   - Medium Gray

Note: You can also change the color by going to User Interface > Workspace Color.

Changing the background color

- Click **View > Background Color** and pick a color of your choice.

You can also change the background color by going to **User Interface > Background Color**.

Using palettes

Different palettes in PaintShop Pro organize data and directions to help you change the way your photos look. Some panels will show up right away when you start a certain tool, while others won't show up until you open them. You can quickly turn on and off a palette by choosing View Palettes. You can only get to some images from certain tabs. On panels, which may also have command buttons and controls, information is shown. Like toolbars, palettes can be moved from where they normally stay.

Below are the available palette and its description:

- **Brush Variance**: Customize brush settings for precise control, especially useful with pressure-sensitive tablets or four-dimensional mice.
- **Histogram**: Analyze image color and tonal distribution to guide corrections in shadows, mid-tones, and highlights.
- **History**: Track and undo actions performed on the image.
- **Info Palette**: View and edit image details like settings, tags, and location.
- **Instant Effects**: Easily apply preset effects to your images.
- **Layers**: Manage and adjust parameters for image layers.
- **Learning Center**: Access detailed instructions and assistance for various tasks.
- **Materials:** Choose colors and materials for painting and retouching.
- **Mixer**: Create realistic oil paint strokes with pigment mixing tools.
- **Overview**: View a thumbnail of the image, zoom options, and details.
- **Organizer**: Manage and edit images from multiple folders, and customize trays for workflow.

- **Script Output**: Review actions and outcomes after running scripts.

To manage palettes and toolbars:

- **Display palettes**: Access palettes from the View menu or by hitting F2, resize by dragging corners or edges.
- **Use toolbars**: Access various toolbars for editing, effects, scripts, file management, painting, and more from the Edit tab.
- **Tooltip and status bar**: Get additional information about toolbar buttons and tools by hovering over them, and receive further instructions from the Learning Center.

These features streamline editing tasks and offer efficient ways to enhance and manage your images.

How to make a toolbar visible or invisible

- **Show or hide toolbars**: Navigate to View > Toolbars and select or deselect the toolbar names. A check mark indicates the toolbar is active. Additionally, right-clicking any toolbar in the Edit tab allows you to access and toggle toolbars. Click the Close button on a toolbar's title bar to hide it.

To use tools effectively:

- **Utilize tooltips and status bar**: Hover over a tool to see its name and shortcut key in a tooltip. The status bar provides further tips and information when a tool is selected.
- **Access tools**: Most picture creation and editing tools are available through the Edit tab. Some, like Crop, Move, and Text tools, are located on the Tools toolbar. Tools are often grouped with related activities indicated by a flyout arrow.
- **Consider layer compatibility**: Certain tools, like Paint Brush and Clone Brush, are only functional on raster layers. Others, such as the Pen tool, work exclusively on vector layers.

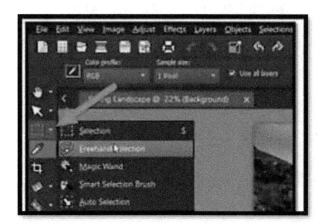

Starting a new Project

1. **Launch PaintShop Pro**: Start by opening Corel PaintShop Pro on your computer. You can do this by double-clicking the desktop shortcut or by searching for the program in the Start menu (Windows) or the Applications folder (macOS).

2. **Create a New Project**: Once PaintShop Pro is open, navigate to the "File" menu at the top left corner of the screen. Click on "File" and then select "New" from the drop-down menu. Alternatively, you can use the keyboard shortcut Ctrl + N (Cmd + N on macOS) to create a new project.

3. **Set Project Properties**: A new dialog box will appear, allowing you to set the properties for your new project. Here, you can specify details such as the dimensions (width and height) of your project in pixels, inches, or other units, as well as the resolution. You can also choose whether to start with a transparent background or a specific color background.

4. **Choose a Template (Optional)**: If you prefer, you can select a pre-designed template for your project from the Template Library. Simply click on the "Templates" tab in the New dialog box and browse through the available templates. Choose the one that best fits your project idea and click "OK" to proceed.

5. **Customize Settings (Optional)**: Depending on your project requirements, you may want to customize additional settings before starting. For example, you can adjust the color depth, background type, and other advanced options. Take your time to explore these settings and make any necessary adjustments.

6. **Begin Creating**: Once you've set up your project properties and any optional settings, click "OK" to create your new project. You'll now be presented with a blank canvas or workspace, ready for you to start adding elements, editing photos, or creating graphics.

7. **Save Your Project**: Before you dive into your creative process, it's important to save your project. Go to the "File" menu and select "Save As" (or use the shortcut Ctrl + Shift + S / Cmd + Shift + S on macOS). Choose a location on your computer to save the project file, give it a descriptive name, and click "Save."

8. **Get Creative**: With your project set up and saved, it's time to let your creativity flow! Use the various tools, brushes, effects, and features in Corel PaintShop Pro to bring your vision to life. Experiment with different techniques, explore new ideas and enjoy the process of creating something unique.

CHAPTER 3
TRANSFER PICTURES TO OTHER APPLICATIONS

The average file size of digital photos has grown because more and more people have access to high-resolution digital cameras and scanners. When these pictures are moved to the Windows Clipboard, they use a lot more memory than when they are pasted into another program. Using the Copy Special method is the best way to put picture data on the Clipboard so that you can copy it into office programs like word processors, presentation software, and email programs. You can find these steps in the Edit menu.

Make a copy of your photographs to use in other applications

1. Go to **Edit** > **Copy Special** to begin.
2. **Find the following commands in the Copy Special submenu and choose one:**
   - If you choose Copy for Professional Printing, a 300-dpi copy of the present picture on the clipboard is made.
   - For desktop printing, press "Copy for Desktop Printing." This will copy the picture to the clipboard at a size of 200 dots per inch.
   - Copy for Screen or Email copies the picture to the clipboard at 96 dots per inch. You can get this option if you right-click on the picture. It's important to note that all three of these steps in the submenu change the picture depth right away to 8 bits per channel RGB and flatten the image so it only has one layer.
3. Put your mouse on the program you want to put the picture into and press the Ctrl and V keys at the same time.
4. Select **File** > **Save for Office** if you want more options for changing the size of pictures and the type of file they will be saved in when you send them to other programs.

Importing Images

Manage Tab

1. Navigate to the Navigation palette and click on the Collections tab.
2. Select "**Browse More Folders**."
3. In the **Browse for Folder** dialog box, navigate to the desired folder containing your photos.
4. Click OK.

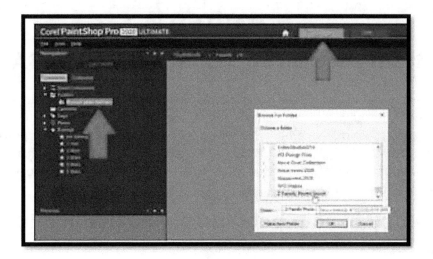

Your selected folder will be added to the folder list, and all images within it will be cataloged in the application database for easy access, editing, and updating.

Scanning images into PaintShop Pro

Edit tab

1. Connect your scanner to your computer and install the accompanying software.
2. In PaintShop Pro, navigate to File > Import, then select "From Scanner or Camera" (WIA option) or "TWAIN Acquire" based on your scanner type.
3. Utilize the scanner's software to conduct the scan.

Once the scanning process is complete, the scanned image will appear in PaintShop Pro. You can choose to continue scanning or exit the scanner's software as needed.

Zoom and Pan

There is a level of zoom in PaintShop Pro that lets you see the whole picture on the desktop when you open an image. This is the setting that comes with it. The image information can be seen better when you zoom in, or the whole picture can be seen better when you zoom out. You can also make a part of a picture bigger. You can see parts of the picture that aren't shown in the window you're currently looking through. When you're working at a high magnification level, you can move to a different part of the picture without changing the magnification level. This makes it possible for you to work faster. When a picture is too big to fit in its window, scroll bars will show up on the bottom and right sides.

How to zoom

1. Select the **Zoom tool** from the "Tools" bar.
2. To make the area bigger, click it. To make it smaller, right-click it. The new magnification

level, which is a percentage that was already set, is shown in the Zoom (%) option on the Tool Options panel.

You also have the option to:

- **Make the picture bigger by a certain percentage:** Enter the number you want to use in the Zoom (%) box on the Tool Options panel.
- **Display the picture in its full size:** Click the **"Zoom to 100%"** option under the Tool Options menu or go to **View > Zoom to 100%.**

The window that shows the picture when you zoom in or out will automatically change its size to fit the new view. If your mouse or pen has a scroll wheel, you can use it to change the size of the image when the Zoom tool is selected. If you go to the menu bar and choose **View > Zoom in** or **View > Zoom out,** you can change how much a picture magnifies.

How to enlarge a portion of a photograph

1. Go to the View menu and select the **Magnifier option** to turn on the magnification mode.
2. Move the mouse to the part of the picture you want to see well. The size shown for the area under the cursor is 500%.
3. To get out of the magnifier mode, go back to the menu bar and select **View > Magnifier** again.

Pan around your image

1. Choose the **"Pan" tool** from the "Tools" bar.

2. Use the mouse to move the picture around.

You also have the option to:

- **Pan while using another tool:** Hold down the Spacebar and drag with the other tool.
- **Use the Overview palette to navigate around a picture:** You can move the preview box on the overview palette to a different spot by dragging it.

Fit window to image

- Pick **"Fit Image"** from the Window menu.

If you have the Pan or Zoom tool chosen, you can also use the Fit Window to Image button on the Tool Options panel to make the window fit the picture.

Undo and redo your actions

If you make changes to a picture, you can undo one action or many actions at once. You can take back changes you've made to the picture, like brushstrokes, color changes, or effects you've added. There are options to redo one action or many actions to follow directions again after undoing them. There is also an option to go back to the last saved state of the picture. Using the History palette, you can undo and redo actions in a certain way, regardless of the order in which they were done. **Note:** Changing the name of a file, saving it, opening and closing it, clearing the clipboard, making changes that affect the whole program (like changing the color settings and preferences), and using commands that don't change the pixels of the image (like zooming or scrolling) can't be undone with the undo button.

Controls for redo and undo are located on the History palette

You can undo more than one action at once with the History palette. The History palette shows all the changes that have been made to the picture that is currently selected. The action that was done first can be found at the very bottom of the list, while the action that was done most recently can be found at the very top of it. The History palette is different from the Undo and Redo controls because it lets you choose to undo or redo actions regardless of the order in which they were done. In the History palette, you can see a list of the 250 most recent commands that were run on the current image. This is the setting that comes with it. The Undo settings can be changed, and you can pick a different amount of undo instructions.

The controls for undoing and redoing previous actions on the History palette are outlined below:

- **Undo to Here:** Any acts that came after the action that was asked for are both undone when you use the Undo to Here action. It will do the same thing when you click this button as when you click the eye icon next to an item. The tasks that haven't been finished are shown in a blank box.
- **Redo to Here:** When you use the Redo to Here function, you undo both the action you chose and any actions that came before it that were not yet done. It will be the same as clicking the eye sign with the yellow X if you click this button.
- **Undo Selected**: You can undo the move that was chosen with the **"Undo Selected"** function. When you click this button, it does the same thing as when you hold down the Control key and click an item's eye icon. Keep in mind that undoing one action could affect other actions and cause results that were not meant or planned.
- **Redo Selected:** If you click on **"Redo Selected,"** you can undo the move you chose. If you held down the Control key and clicked the red X-eye icon next to an item, this button would do the same thing.
- **Clear Commands That Were Selected to Be Undone:** You can clear commands that were chosen to be undone. This turns all actions that were chosen to be undone into commands that can't be undone or redone once they've been changed. It's being asked of you to confirm that you want to do this.
- **Display Commands That Cannot Be Undone:** The commands that can't be undone are shown or hidden. When they are shown, things that can't be undone have a gray background.
- **History of an Empty Command:** This command turns everything in the History palette into a command that can't be undone. It's being asked of you to confirm that you want to do this.

Undo action

- Click on **Edit** and then **Undo** in the menu bar.

To undo more than one thing at once, just press the **Edit | Undo command** more than once. The Undo command lets you undo several actions at once, in the same order that they were done. You can undo certain acts by using the History palette. If the move in question cannot be undone, the "undo" command will not work. You can also select an action from the Standard menu, click the Undo button, or press the Control key and the Z key to undo what you did.

Redo action

- To redo a move, go to **Edit > Redo**.

The Redo command undoes several actions in the same order that they were undone. The Undo command undoes a single action. Using the History palette, you can redo certain acts or parts of them. It is not possible to redo actions unless they have first been undone. You can also undo what you did by hitting **Ctrl + Alt + Z** or by clicking the Redo button on the Standard toolbar.

Revert to the most recent picture version that you saved

- Go to **File > Revert**.

Undo and redo actions by using the History palette

Simply select an action on the History palette, and carry out any of the below options:

- **Undo an action:** If you want to undo what you just did, you can click the Undo/Redo button or the **Undo to Here** option. The tasks that haven't been finished are shown in a blank box.
- **Redo an undone action:** Either click the Undo/Redo button or the Redo to Here button to undo or redo the action that is currently chosen. The actions you have chosen and all the ones that came before them are redone, and their icons will no longer be blank. Keep in mind that actions that were selectively undone (shown by a gray X) before you clicked on the action will not be redone again. The only way to undo these actions is to use the Redo Selected command.
- **Undo a specific part of an activity:** You can either hold down the Control key and click the Undo/Redo button for the move you want to undo, or you can click the **Undo Selected button**. Actions that have been deliberately undone are shown by a gray X.
- **Perform again an action that was only partially undone:** Choose an action and hold down the Ctrl key. Then, click the Undo/Redo button for that action, or click the Redo Selected button.

Set your Undo preferences

1. From the menu bar, choose "**File**," "**Preferences**," and "**General Program Preferences.**"
2. Select "**Undo**" from the list of options on the left.
3. Before moving on, make sure that the box that says "**Enable the undo system**" is checked. For any changes you make to pictures that are already open, you will need to make sure

this box is checked. If the box is not checked after clicking OK in the Preferences dialog box, you will not be able to undo any changes you made to an open picture.

4. **Check the following boxes to indicate your selection or de-select them:**
   - You can choose how much hard disk space is used for undo and redo operations by entering or setting a number in the control. You can set a limit on how much data is used for undo and redo for each open picture. How much storage room is available depends on what is going on at the moment. This option is not required if you have a lot of free space on your disk.
   - The "Limit undo/redo to n steps per open image" setting can be changed from its usual value of 250 steps. There should be more than 500 megabytes of free space on your drive before you change the number on the control.
   - You can set the Redo order to run as quickly as possible by selecting "Enable Fast Redo." Remove this option before using the Undo command if you want it to work as quickly as possible.

5. Type or set a number in the list of **"non-undoable steps"** in the History Palette control. When the limit for undoing and redoing has been met, this value shows how many non-undoable steps are kept. These are steps that can't be undone or redone. In this case, the number 10 is used.

Non-undoable steps can't be redone or undone. Still, they can be used again on the current picture or other open pictures that have been saved to a QuickScript or regular PSScript file or copied to the Clipboard.

Repeat a command

The Repeat command lets you use an effect or fix it again after you've already used it, so you don't have to go back to the relevant text box every time. The most recent command that can be used again will always be shown in the Edit menu. If the previous command cannot be repeated, the Repeat command will not be given.
   - Select **Edit > Repeat**.

You can give the same orders more than once by writing them down in a script and then running that script on each picture. You can also do something again by holding down Shift and clicking on any button or item in the menu. It is the most recent choice that is used when you use the repeated command.

Delete images

Using the Organizer palette, you can remove image files from your computer.

   - Right-click on a picture in the Organizer palette and pick Delete from the menu that comes up. This will get rid of the image that was chosen.

Supported Files

As you can see from the table below, PaintShop Pro can open the following file types. There is an asterisk (*) next to the file format name, which means that only the 32-bit version of the program can read or write to that file format.

EPS	Encapsulated PostScript	Read/Write
ERF	Epson RAW	Read only
GEM	Ventura/GEM Drawing	Read only
GIF	Compuserve Graphics Interchange	Read/Write
HDP	HD Photo format	Read/Write
HEIC	High Efficiency Image Format (HEIF). HEIC is the extension used for the container file.	Read only
HPGL*, HGL*, HPG*	HP Graphics Language	Read only

Format	Description	Support
3FR	Hasselblad RAW	Read only
AI	Adobe Illustrator	Read/Write
ARW	Sony RAW	Read only
BMP	Windows Bitmap	Read/Write
CAL	CALS Raster	Read/Write
CGM	Computer Graphics Metafile	Read only
CLP	Windows Clipboard	Read/Write
CR2	Canon RAW	Read only
CRW	Canon RAW	Read only
CT	PaintShop Pro graphics	Read/Write
CUR	Windows Cursor	Read only
CUT	Dr. Halo	Read/Write
DCR	Kodak RAW	Read only
DCX	Zsoft Multipage Paintbrush	Read only
DIB	Windows DIB	Read/Write
DNG	Adobe Digital Negative	Read only
DRW*	Micrografx Draw	Read only
EMF	Windows Enhanced Metafile	Read/Write

IFF	Amiga	Read/Write
IMG	GEM Paint	Read/Write
J2C	JPEG 2000	Read/Write
J2K	JPEG 2000	Read/Write
JIF	JPEG	Read/Write
JP2	JPEG 2000	Read/Write
JPG	JPEG – JFIF Compliant	Read/Write
JPS	Stereo JPEG	Read only
K25	Kodak Digital Camera File	Read only
KDC	Kodak Digital Camera File	Read only
LBM	Deluxe Paint	Read/Write
MAC	MacPaint	Read/Write
MEF	RAW format	Read only
MOS	Leaf RAW Image	Read only
MPO	Multiple Picture Object	Read/Write
MRW	Minolta RAW	Read only
MSP	Microsoft Paint	Read/Write
NEF	Nikon RAW	Read only
NRW	Nikon RAW	Read only

PSD	Photoshop	Read/Write
PspImage	PaintShop Pro Image	Read/Write
PSP	Animation Shop	Read
RAF	Fuji RAW	Read only
RAS	Sun Raster Image	Read/Write
RAW	RAW Graphics File Format	Read/Write
RIFF	Corel Painter	Read/Write
RLE	Windows or CompuServe RLE	Read/Write
RW2	LUMIX RAW	Read only
SCT	SciTex Continous Tone	Read/Write
SR2	Sony RAW	Read only
SRF	Sony RAW	Read only
SVG, SVGZ	Scalable Vector Graphics	Read only
TGA	Truevision Targa	Read/Write
TIF	Tagged Image File Format	Read/Write
UFO	Ulead File Object	Read only
WBM, WBMP	Wireless Bitmap	Read/Write
WDP	Windows Media	Read only
WEBP	WebP Image	Read/Write

Using adjust

Taking lots of pictures with your digital camera is a fun and easy thing to do. At times, though, it can be hard just to read through them all, let alone change them. By clicking on the Adjust tab, you can make this task more fun. You can make basic changes like cropping, straightening, color correction, and getting rid of blemishes and red eyes. You can even give photo ratings and then delete them from your gallery. Thanks to this mode of fast editing, you can quickly make the first cut of photos before focusing on a few to do more detailed work on them.

What is the significance of the Adjust tab?

When you use the Adjust tab, the settings are right in front of you. This makes it easy to get to the PaintShop Pro tools and features you use most often. You can switch to the advanced editing mode, which gives you access to all of the app's tools and features, by clicking the Edit tab at the very top of the app's window. The picture that you saw most recently in the Adjust tab will now be the current picture.

Display the Adjust tab

In Preferences, you can turn on the Adjust tab to see it.

1. Go to the "**File**" menu, then "**Preferences**," and finally "**General Program Preferences.**"
2. Click on the tab for the area you want to see.
3. In the section called "**Visible Tabs**," check the "**Adjust**" box. You will need to choose the option to "**Set Adjust as default**" to make the Adjust tab your default setting.

Activate the Adjust tab

Using the Adjust tab, you can make changes to each picture separately. When you pick a new tool or feature, the changes you made are made right away. Also, the changes can be undone. While editing, you can see the first picture again. When you're done changing one picture, you can quickly move on to the next one by clicking on a thumbnail in the Organizer palette. Autosave can be turned on when asked to save manually, or you can set it to save instantly every time you click a new picture.

Use the Adjust tab on your browser

Choose one of the following actions in the Adjust palette:

- Pick out a tool and change the settings to modify the picture. When you click the "**Apply**" button or select another tool or adjustment option, the changes take effect.
- Click on the name of the adjustment tool you want to use. The screen for changing the settings. The changes take place when you choose a different feature.

Undo changes in the Adjust

Choose one of the subsequent options:

- Pick up the Undo button on the toolbar.
- The **Reset button** is at the bottom of the Adjust box. Click it to undo all the changes you made.

View original image

- In the lower part of the Adjust pane, press and hold the **Show Original button**. Then, release your finger from the button to go back to the version of the image that was changed.

Using depth info to choose areas

As long as your camera saves depth information (XDM metadata), you can use the Adjust tabs Depth Selection feature to change things about certain parts of photos or add Instant Effects. The distance between the things in the picture and a camera's depth sensor tells us how deep the picture is.

Choose a point based on the depth of info

1. Click on the Adjust tab to begin.
2. Use the Navigator tool in the Organizer palette to get to a picture that has depth information.
3. Go to the Adjust panel and click on **Depth Selection**.

4. Check the **Enable Selection box** to show a selection bar.
5. Move the sliders on the Depth Range to set the minimum (Near) and maximum (Far) distances for the selection.
6. **Moving the Size slider will let you pick a brush size. Next, pick one of the options below to make the selection even more refined:**
   - After clicking "Add," drag your mouse around the edges of the Preview area to choose the place you want to select.
   - To remove the selected areas, click **Remove** and move the mouse over them in the Preview area.
   - Make sure the Flip Selection option box is checked if you want to invert the option.

Reviewing, organizing, and finding pictures

The Manage tab has tools that can help you review, organize, and speed up the photo editing process.

Manage tab

When you click on the Manage tab, you can see the Navigation palette, the Preview area, the Organizer palette, and the Info palette. You can change Manage by choosing the Preview or Thumbnail mode, moving, scaling, or hiding the palettes, and changing the display and file settings to suit your needs.

Switch between Preview and Thumbnail modes

Select one of the buttons in the top-right corner from the list below:

- In thumbnail mode, the content of the Organizer palette is locked in the viewing area and made bigger.
- The preview mode shows a big part of a single picture.

Resize Manage tab palettes

1. Move the mouse over the edge of the palette you want to change sizes when the pointer changes into a two-way arrow.
2. To make the area bigger or smaller, just drag it. When you change the layout settings in the Manage tab, the app keeps them and saves them right away for your next session.

Hide or Show the Navigation palette and Information palette

To open the Organizer palette, choose one of the Organizer toolbar buttons by clicking it.

- **Navigation Show/Hide:** This option shows or hides the Navigation palette.
- The Info palette lets you show or hide information about a picture.

To quickly shrink the Organizer palette (or any other palette), all you have to do is click the **Auto Hide button** on the palette's title bar.

Browse folders for your pictures

Using the Collections and Computer tabs in the Navigation panel, you can browse through the photographs on your computer:

- On the Collections tab, you can find both your virtual and actual folder library. As files from the Collections page are added to the catalog, it becomes easy to view and search for favorite photos (this is a type of indexing). This means that you can use file management tools like tags to help you find photos and lists of things and grades. You can add or remove folders from the Collections page at any time.
- Below the computer tab, you can see a full list of all the files on your desktop and hard drive. These tools, like tags, captions, and ratings, can't be used to find or sort photos that you see in the computer tab because they haven't been added to the collection. Why use the tab for the computer? It's easy to get things from somewhere else that you don't want to or can't add to the catalog right now. For example, the computer tab is great if you need to get to a file in a temporary folder or a picture in a folder with a lot of files you don't use very often.

The pictures in the folder are shown as thumbnails in the Organizer palette when the Navigation palette is used to select the folder. People can tell the cataloging process which formats and files they should not include.

How to view the pictures in a folder

1. **In the Navigation palette, pick one of the tabs below:**
   - **Collections**: This feature gives you a unique list of cataloged folders as well as a list of virtual collections.
   - **Computer**: shows a list of all the drives and folders on your machine.
2. Double-click on a folder to see the subfolders it has.
3. Click on the folder that has the pictures you want to see to open it.

The Organizer palette shows thumbnails of all the picture files in the chosen folder that are compatible. By clicking the minus sign next to the name of a folder, you can also hide the list of files that are inside it.

Include a new folder on the collection page

1. Go to the Navigation Palette and click on the **Collections tab**.
2. From the list of folders, choose **Browse More Folders**.
3. Once you've found the folder with the pictures you want to upload, click OK. Make sure you pick a good area because each subdirectory inside it is listed. Adding your folder or a root folder to your computer might start a lot of cataloging that you don't need.

Another way to make a folder on your computer is to choose the **Make New Folder** option in the Browse for Folder dialog box.

Delete the folder from the collection page

1. From the Navigation palette, choose the **Collections tab**.
2. In the Folder list, right-click the folder you want to get rid of.
3. Pick **"Remove from List."**

The images in the folder will still have their file management information (tags, ratings, and captions) even after the folder is removed from the Collections page and the catalog. However, you will no longer be able to look for this information.

View all of the images that have been cataloged

1. Go to the Navigation Palette and click on the **Collections tab**.
2. Choose **"All Photos"** from the list of Smart Collections.

Find images on your PC

When you load photos into PaintShop Pro, they are automatically put into a catalog. You can get to them from the Navigation panel. Real-time filtering makes it easy and quick to look through cataloged photos from the Search box. You can use a calendar, a simple text-based search, or more advanced search tools to find photos that are linked to a certain day or set of dates. As a Smart Collection, you have the option to save the search criteria and results from an advanced search.

Perform a fast search for photos

Type a search word into the box that says "Search" on the navigation bar.

Note: Keywords for searches can be tags, caption text, filenames (including extensions), folder names (including drive-designating letters), or picture data (EXIF or IPTC data).

To do an advanced search:

1. Go to the Navigation Palette and click on the **Collections tab**.
2. Double-click Smart Collections to open the list, and then click **Add Smart Collection**. The Smart Collection text box shows up.
3. From the list of choices labeled **Find photographs that match,** pick one of the following:
   - **All:** Look for pictures that follow all the rules that have been set out.
   - **Any:** Look for pictures that meet any of the requirements given.
4. Choose a search option from the first drop list on the left.
5. Pick a search option from the list below to make your search even more specific. Different options will show up in the drop-down menu depending on the search option you chose

in the last one.

6. Type a search word into the box or choose one. **Note**: The search word you type in must match the search option you pick from the first drop-down menu in the search rule. If you pick Rating, click on the number of stars that shows how the picture was rated.

7. Click on Preview.

    - **Add a search rule:** Click the "**Add Rule**" button in the upper right corner of the window.
    - **Remove or delete the last search rule:** Just click on the button that says "**Remove Rule.**"
    - **Save the search as a Smart Collection:** Click Save in the Smart Collection box. In the Save as Smart Collection box, give it a name and click "Save." This group can be found in the list of Smart Collections.

Work with previously saved search

If you save a unique set of search terms as a Smart Collection, you can easily run a search again by clicking on it in the Collections menu. You can also change, rename, or get rid of a saved search.

Run saved search

1. Go to the Navigation Palette and click on the **Collections tab**.
2. Double-click **Smart Collections** to see the list.
3. Pick the Smart Collection you want to use to begin your search.

Edit saved search

1. Go to the Navigation Palette and click on the **Collections tab**.
2. Double-click **Smart Collections** to see the list.
3. From the smart collection's menu, choose **Edit** from the drop-down menu.
4. Change the search terms, and then click on Preview. The search results are shown in the Organizer palette.
5. Click "Save." The search term stands out in the Save as Smart Collection dialog box's text field.
6. Press "Save" one more time. In the text box, give the new search a name. Then, click Save to keep the old search from being overwritten.

Rename the search that was saved

1. From the Navigation palette, choose the **Collections tab.**
2. Double-click **Smart Collections** to see the list.
3. Use the Smart Collection's context menu to choose "**Rename.**" In the Rename Smart Collection dialog box that shows up, the search word is highlighted.
4. Type in a new name and then click "Save."

Remove any stored searches

1. From the Navigation palette, choose the **Collections tab.**
2. Double-click **Smart Collections** to see the list.
3. Choose the Smart Collection from the menu that pops up and click "**Delete**."

You should include keyword tags with your photos

Using keyword tags, you can give picture labels that are useful and easy to understand. By adding tags like "**family,**" "**children,**" or "**birthday**," you can identify certain pictures. Then, you can choose a tag from the list to see thumbnails of photos that have that tag. You can get to your newly made tags from the Navigation palette, which is where the tags library is located. There are no limits on how many tags you can add to a picture.

Add the keywords tab in the catalog of tags

1. From the Navigation palette, choose the **Collections tab**.
2. Click **Tags** once more to see the list.
3. In the list of tags, click the "**Add Tags**" button.
4. Type the words for the tag, and then click OK. The new tag is now on the list of Tags.

Delete the tags for terms straight from the tags catalog

1. From the Navigation palette, choose the **Collections tab**.
2. Click **Tags** once more to see the list.
3. Right-click on a tag and choose "**Delete**."

Remove keyword tags from images

1. Pick one or more thumbnails from the Organizer palette.
2. Go to the Info palette and select the **General tab** to see the tag details.
3. From the list below the Tags box, click one or more of the tags you want to remove. Then, click the **Delete Tag button** to the right of the tag name.
4. If you can't see the Info palette already, click the **Image information button** on the Organizer menu to open it.

View your pictures by tags

After you describe a tag with a picture, you can easily find it by clicking on the tag.

Display your pictures by tags

1. From the Navigation palette, choose the **Collections tab**.
2. Click **Tags** once more to see the list.
3. Pick a tag. In the Organizer palette, you can see images of the photos that go with the tag.

You can also type a tag name in the Search field at the top of the Navigation palette. In the tags list, you can also click the "**No Tags**" button to see pictures that don't have any tags.

Adding Tags and Metadata for Efficient Organization

To add a keyword tag:
1. Navigate to Organizer/Manage Mode and go to the Collections tab in the Navigation panel.
2. Click the plus button next to Tags to reveal the tags controls and the list of available tags.
3. Within the Tags list, click the Add Tags button.
4. Enter the desired tag text and click OK. The new tag will be nested under Tags in the Collections tab of the Navigation panel.

To delete a keyword tag:
1. Again, in Organizer/Manage Mode, access the Collections tab in the Navigation panel.
2. Click the plus button next to Tags to display the list of available tags.
3. Right-click on the tag you wish to delete from the Tags list.
4. Choose Delete.

To assign a keyword tag to images:
1. In Organizer/Manage Mode, access the Collections tab in the Navigation panel.
2. Click the plus button next to Tags to display the list of available tags.
3. Select one or more thumbnails in the Thumbnails panel that you want to tag.
4. Drag the thumbnails onto the selected tag. Alternatively, assign tags by typing tag text in the Tags section of the General Info panel for selected thumbnails, and then click the Add Tag button beside each tag text field.

To remove keyword tags from one or more images:

Organizer / Manage Mode

1. In the Thumbnails panel, select one or more thumbnails whose tags you want to remove. The General info panel displays information about the last selected image in the sequence.
2. In the Tags box of the General info panel, select one or more tags that you want to remove, and click the **Delete Tag** button

Geo-Tagging Photos in PaintShop Pro

Search Photos by Location and on a Map

1. Open PaintShop Pro and ensure you're in the Manage Workspace.
2. Click on the Map mode option.
3. In the Map View Search box, enter the name of a place or city associated with your photos.

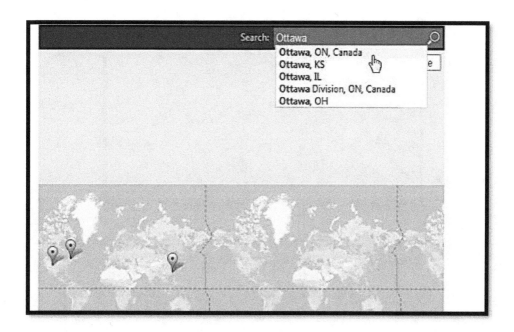

4. If prompted, agree to add the geographical location to all photos in the opened folder.
5. Zoom in on the Map view to the specified location.
6. In the Organizer window, look for a push pin in the lower-right corner of the photo's thumbnail, indicating geotagging.

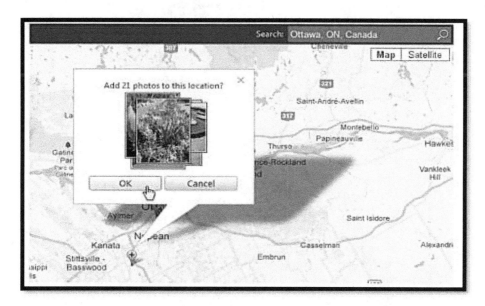

7. To pinpoint specific geotagged photos, zoom in further by dragging the Zoom scroll bar or selecting a geotagged photo.

In areas with Google Maps' 360-degree street view available, drag the human icon to explore the location. Blue lines indicate available Google Street View.

The blue lines that appear on the map when selecting the human icon indicate that Google Street View is available at that location.

Adding Locations to Photos

In this scenario, where photos from Arizona were taken with a camera lacking GPS capabilities, you can manually geotag them in PaintShop Pro to map them to their respective shooting locations.

1. First, select the photos that you wish to use, from the **Organizer**.

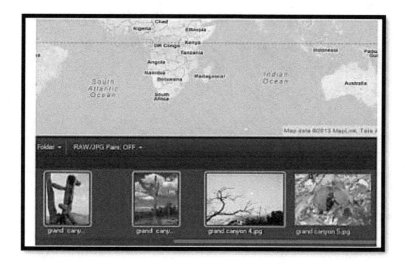

2. Next, locate the area where the photos were shot.

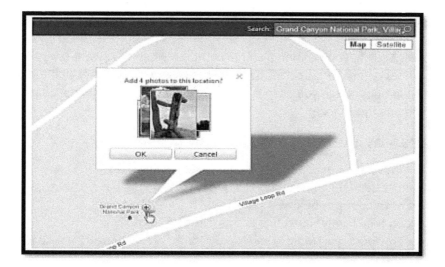

3. Place the push pin to **Geo-Tag** the photos.

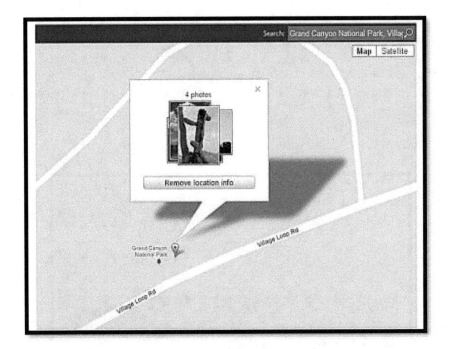

Changing or Removing Locations of Photos

1. Select the photos.
2. Remove the existing geotag.
3. Place the push pin on the correct location on the map to geotag the photos.
4. Adjust the push pin if needed for precise tagging.

Make use of the calendar to find your photographs

With the Calendar Search, you can find pictures based on when they were taken. You can either pick a range of dates or look for a specific date. On the calendar, the times that the pictures were taken are shown in bold. When you change and save a picture, the Calendar Search keeps track of the date you made the change.

Find pictures by utilizing a calendar

1. Go to the Navigation Palette and click on the **Collections tab**.
2. Click on the **calendar icon**. Pictures that were made on the dates shown in red are shown.
3. **Pick one of the options below:**
   - Click on the "**Today**" button to see pictures taken today.
   - Click Previous (Year/Month) and Next (Month/Year), then pick a date to find a certain year, month, and day.
   - To choose a set of dates, use the **Previous and Next buttons** to click on the month

and year. Hold down Shift and click on the first date in the range. Then click on the last date in the range.

- Use the Previous and Next keys to choose the month and year, then hold down the Ctrl key and click on the dates. This will select several dates that are not in order. When you click on a date or set of dates, the Organizer palette shows thumbnails of the photos that belong to that date.

4. You can close the Calendar Search box by clicking the Close button.

Working with thumbnails in the Manage tab

The Manage tab's thumbnails make it easy to see what your photos will look like and arrange them. To see photos in full-screen mode for a better look, use the Preview mode, the thumbnail zoom-in and out settings, or Quick Review. The thumbnails can be sorted by name, date, or grade, among other things. With thumbnails, you can also rotate the pictures, delete files, and change their names. When you take several pictures, you can use Auto Group and RAW/JPG Pairings to combine and show thumbnails that follow the choices for bracketing or JPEG+RAW file pairs. Using the Capture editing and Apply editing tools, you can change many photos at once by using previews. There are also options to pick one or more views for RAW files and change the format of the files.

Zoom in or out on thumbnails

1. It's in the top right corner of the Manage tab. If it's not already there, click the **Thumbnail mode button.**
2. You can zoom in or out by moving the Zoom slider on the Organizer toolbar to the left or right.

Note: You can't use the Zoom tool when the Manage tab is in Preview mode.

Organize your thumbnails

1. Choose "**Sort by**" from the Organizer toolbar's drop-down menu.
2. Choose a sorting method.
3. **Pick one of the options below:**
   - Date Modified sorts previews by the date that the picture was last changed. The folder sorts images by folder name in alphabetical order.
   - Filename sorts images by filename in ascending order.
   - Date Created—Newest sorts thumbnails by the date they were taken, from most recent to oldest.
   - Date Created— Oldest sorts pictures by the date they were taken, from oldest to newest.
   - **File Format:** thumbnails are sorted by file format in alphabetical order.
   - **Rating:** Sorts thumbnails by picture ratings, like ".psp image," ".jpg," or ".tif."
   - **File Size:** This option sorts images by file size (in kilobytes), from smallest to largest.

- **Position**—sets thumbnails in order based on where the picture was taken;

Rating organizes thumbnails based on the ratings given to each picture

When you open the Organizer menu, choose Auto Group and then set a time range. Because of this, pictures taken during that time are shown as sets, with lines between them.

Adjust the way that JPEG and RAW pairing are displayed

Select one of the following alternatives by clicking the RAW/JPEG Pairs button on the Organizer toolbar:

- ON - Show JPEG Versions: When this setting is turned on, the RAW versions are hidden and the JPEG versions are shown as previews.
- ON - Show RAW Versions: When this setting is turned on, the JPEG versions are hidden and the RAW versions are shown as previews.
- OFF—Shows previews of the RAW and JPEG versions of the files.

It is possible for both copies of a file to be sent to the recycle bin if the RAW/JPEG Pairs option is turned on.

Pick more than just a thumbnail to see

Choose one of the subsequent options:

- Hold down Shift and click the first and last thumbnails in the list to select thumbnails that are next to each other.
- Click pictures that are not next to each other while holding down Ctrl to select them.

Rotate photos in the Organizer palette

1. Pick out a few pictures.
2. Click on any of the following buttons on the Organizer toolbar:
   - **Rotate Right:** images can be turned 90 degrees clockwise.
   - **Rotate Left:** The images are turned 90 degrees counterclockwise.

If you right-click on a picture, you can also use the menu that appears to choose either Rotate Right or Rotate Left.

Erase more than one picture in Manage

1. Select one or more images and press the **Delete** key.

2. Select "**Yes**" to send the pictures to the trash.

Note: You can also get rid of pictures by selecting a thumbnail, right-clicking it, and selecting "Delete" from the menu that appears.

Rename files in the Manage tab

1. Right-click on the file's thumbnail and choose "**Rename**" from the menu that comes up.
2. In the Rename File box, type the new name for the file, and then click OK.

Open more than one image for advanced editing

- Pick out a few pictures, and then click on the Edit tab.
- You can also open the Edit tab by right-clicking on one or more thumbnails and picking Edit Photo from the menu that appears.

Capture and apply edits to several pictures

You can copy the changes you make to one photo and use them on as many other pictures as you want. As an example, it's easy to quickly use the same border and scale options on a group of photos you're making for a website. When you make changes to a picture in Edit, a small changing icon appears on the thumbnail. When you go back to Manage, you can use the Capture editing and Apply editing options to get other photos to copy the changes you made. You can record and change most files types, but you can only change other RAW files while editing RAW files. You can undo any changes you make to one or more pictures.

Capture edits

1. Save any changes you make to an image.
2. In the Organizer palette, pick out the thumbnail of the picture you changed. In the top left corner of the thumbnail, a pencil or RAW icon will show up if the image has been changed.
3. Click the Capture Editing button on the organizer panel. You can only save changes that are made to files that are open or closed at the moment. When the program is stopped, all changes that were made are erased right away. When you right-click on the picture you want to record, you can choose Capture Editing from the menu that comes up.

Apply captured edits

1. Pick one or more pictures from the Organizer palette.
2. Click the **Apply Editing button** on the Organizer toolbar.
3. Click OK in the Batch Progress box.

For RAW files, the stored settings in the Camera RAW Lab dialog box are used. When you close the program, it erases all of your changes instantly. By right-clicking on the thumbnails you want to use and choosing "Apply Editing," you can also use the changes that were recorded.

Undo Apply Editing

1. Pick one or more pictures from the Organizer palette.
2. Right-click on a picture and a menu will appear. Choose "Revert Current Editing" from that menu.

You can undo changes you made to more than one picture by selecting the thumbnails of those photos, right-clicking on one of them, and choosing "**Revert All Editing**" from the menu that appears.

Displaying and modifying photo information

The Manage tab has an Info palette where you can see, adds, and change information about your pictures. This includes the filename, size, creation date, and EXIF and IPTC metadata. You can also rate pictures with stars, add tags, and write captions. Adding and updating picture information makes it easier to find photos and put them in order. For example, you can use captions to find information. Using the camera-style display at the top of the Info palette, you can quickly look over the camera settings and lens that were used on the chosen shot. Organizer has a button called "**Image Information**" that you can use to show or hide the information palette. You can choose whether to show or hide the Info palette by default based on how much room you need.

Apply a rating to several different pictures

1. Pick out a few pictures.
2. To give it a rating, click on a star in the Info palette and move your mouse from left to right. Say you want to give something five stars, click on the star that is closest to the right.

In addition:

- **Use the context menu to give a rating:** From the context menu, choose one or more images, click Set Rating, and then click the number of stars you want to give each one.
- **Assign a rating by using keyboard shortcuts:** Pick out one or more pictures, then press Ctrl + however many stars you want. For example, press Ctrl + 1 to give one star.

Remove image rating

To change an image's star grade, right-click on a thumbnail and choose "**Set Rating**." If you choose Set Rating * * *, for example, you can uncheck the box next to an image's three-star rating.

Caption images

1. Pick out one or more pictures.

2. Go to the Info palette and click on the **General** tab. Then, type something in the Caption

box.

Take out the captions from the images

1. Pick one or more images that all have the same caption text.
2. Select the **General tab** from the list of options.
3. In the Caption box, click on the words you want to get rid of.
4. Press the **delete** key.

View further picture information

In the info box, click on either the **EXIF or IPTC tab**. You can see the EXIF or IPTC data for the picture. Remember that you can only change EXIF or IPTC data that has input fields.

Utilize Quick Review to go through images

You can use Quick Review to look over photos in full-screen mode. For example, you can quickly look through all the photos you've saved from your camera, delete the ones you don't want, rotate the photos, and rate them with stars using Quick Check.

Examine the photographs in full-screen mode

1. In the Organizer palette, double-click on a thumbnail of the folder or tray you want to look at.
2. **Pick a task from the list below.**
   - **View the following image:** Click on the "**Next Image**" button.
   - **View the earlier picture:** Pick it to see the previous picture.
   - **Open the photo in Edit:** Choose "**Edit Photo**" from the menu.
   - **Give it a star rating:** To rate the picture, click on one of the stars below it, going from left to right.
   - **Zoom level adjustment:** To change the zoom level, click the Zoom in or Zoom out button, the Zoom to 100% button, the Zoom to Window button, or the Zoom scale.

Trays

You can use trays to put pictures from different folders together. The pictures are still where they belong, even though they are listed in the tray and can be reached by clicking on a thumbnail. You can name, delete, and add trays to make your work run better. You can put photos in a tray that you want to edit, use for a project, print, or email, for example. Trays can be made in the Organizer palette. At the moment, the photos from the folder or collection you selected in the Navigation palette are shown in the usual tray. A custom tray, called My Tray, is a blank tray that is made automatically.

Add Tray

1. In the Organizer menu, click More Options and then click Add Tray to start up the

Organizer palette.

2. Give the new tray a name in the Name field, and then click OK.

Rename a tray

1. In the Organizer palette, pick out the tray you want to change the name of.
2. To change the name of the tray, go to the More Options menu on the Organizer panel and choose it.
3. Give the tray a new name in the Name field, and then press OK.

Take out the tray

1. In the Organizer palette, pick out the tray you want to get rid of. Removing a tray does not get rid of the pictures that are on it.
2. The More Options on the Organizer toolbar can be used to get rid of the tray.

Other steps:

1. To start, click on a tray in the Organizer palette.
2. Pick out the pictures you want to get rid of.
3. Press the delete key.

Put photographs on the trays

1. From the Organizer palette, pick out the thumbnails of the photos you want to add to the tray.
2. Right-click on a picture and choose "Add to Tray." You can now find the pictures in My Tray.
3. To add pictures to a custom tray, select the images and drag them to the custom tray tab in the Organizer palette.

Save the items in a tray to a folder

1. Go to the Navigation Palette and click on the Collections tab.
2. Click Browse More Folders and then select **Make New Folder** to select the desired location
3. Name the folder and then click OK.
4. Press Ctrl + A to pick all the pictures in a tray in the Organizer palette.
5. Put the pictures in the new folder.

Organizing Images

1. **Organize Folders:** Arrange images into folders based on categories or projects using your computers file explorer or PaintShop Pro's Organizer.
2. **Import Images:** Import images into PaintShop Pro from organized folders using the Organizer or directly from your computer.

3. **Tag and Keyword:** Add metadata to images by tagging and keywording them, enabling easy search and filtering.
4. **Rate and Sort:** Assign ratings and sort images based on criteria like date, name, rating, or tags to quickly find desired images.
5. **Create Collections:** Group related images into virtual collections or albums within PaintShop Pro, maintaining organization without moving files.
6. **Backup and Archive:** Regularly backup image files to prevent data loss, considering external drives, cloud storage, or archival solutions for safekeeping.

Organizing Images into Folders and Albums

1. **Create Folders**:
   - Open Corel PaintShop Pro and navigate to the Organizer workspace.
   - In the Organizer, locate the "Folders" panel on the left side of the screen.
   - Right-click within the Folders panel and select "New Folder."
   - Name your new folder according to your desired category or project (e.g., "Family Photos," "Vacation 2023," "Work Projects").
   - Repeat this process to create additional folders as needed to organize your images.
2. **Import Images into Folders**:
   - After creating folders, you can import images directly into them.
   - Locate the folder in the Folders panel where you want to import your images.
   - Right-click on the folder and select "Import" from the context menu.
   - Choose the images you want to import from your computer and click "Open" to import them into the selected folder.
3. **Create Albums**:
   - Albums in PaintShop Pro are virtual collections that allow you to organize and group images without moving them from their original folders.
   - To create an album, go to the "Albums" tab in the Organizer workspace.
   - Click on the "+" icon or right-click within the Albums panel and select "New Album."
   - Give your album a descriptive name (e.g., "Best of 2023," "Portrait Shots," "Travel Memories").
   - Once the album is created, you can add images to it by dragging and dropping photos from your folders or by selecting images and using the "Add to Album" option.
4. **Organize Images within Albums**:
   - Once you've added images to an album, you can rearrange them as needed.
   - Click on the album in the Albums panel to view its contents.
   - Drag and drop images within the album to change their order or group them logically.
5. **Utilize Tags and Keywords**:

- In addition to folders and albums, you can use tags and keywords to further organize and categorize your images.
- Select one or more images in the Organizer and click on the "Keywords" tab.
- Add relevant tags and keywords to your images to make them easily searchable.

6. **Backup and Maintenance**:
   - Regularly back up your image library to ensure that your photos are safe and secure.
   - Perform routine maintenance tasks such as deleting duplicates, organizing new images into folders, and updating album contents to keep your photo library tidy and manageable.

CHAPTER 4
CORRECT PHOTOGRAPHIC PERSPECTIVE

Tall or wide things can cause perspective distortion, which makes it look like something is leaning or tilted. This distortion takes place when the camera is pointed at the subject at an angle. The Perspective Correction tool can fix perspective distortions like the way the sides of a building are tilted. You can change the view of a whole layer with the Pick tool.

Correct perspective in photos

1. Choose the **Perspective Correction tool** from the list of tools on the toolbar.

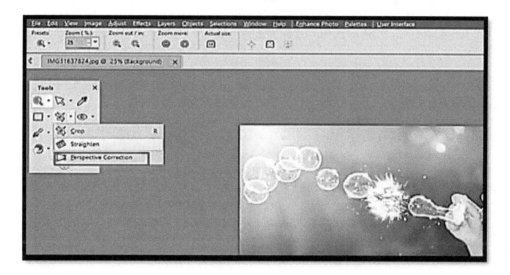

2. **Change the values for the following controls in the Tool Options palette:**
   - **Grid lines**: You can type in or set the number of gridlines you want.
   - **Crop picture:** The picture is cropped out again, this time in a rectangular shape after perspective is applied.

Note: To get rid of the parts of the picture that are outside the rectangle, you need to check the Crop image box.

3. Move each handle to a corner of the rectangle-shaped thing.
4. Choose "**Apply**" from the list.

The order will also be carried out by double-clicking the picture. If you go to the Tool Options panel and click "**Cancel**," the perspective correction box will change back to its original square shape.

Precise perspective in the imaging layer

1. In the Layers panel, pick the layer that needs to be fixed.
2. Click on **View Grid** to see the gridlines.

Using the gridlines, you can change lines in your pictures that should be straight or wavy. When View Change Grid, Guide & Snap Properties are chosen, the tools on the Grid page of the dialog box can be used to change the grid's settings.

3. On the Tools bar, choose the Pick tool. It can be helpful to make the picture window bigger so that you can see all of the corner handles for the present layer. To make the picture view bigger, drag from the corner or the side.
4. Hold down Ctrl and drag a corner handle on the layer you chose. The picture changes when you let go of the pressure. You should change the viewpoint until the picture looks right.

Note: If the fix leaves some picture data outside the image canvas, you can get it back by making the canvas bigger.

Perform fundamental alterations to the image mechanically

If you're not sure what will look best, you can use either the One Step Photo Fix or the Smart Photo Fix tool to change a picture. When you choose the "One Step Shot Fix" command, your picture will automatically get a certain set of color balance and sharpening changes. If you want to change the same fixes before you use them, use the Smart Photo Fix command.

Apply basic corrections using Single/One Step Photo Fix

*   Choose **One Step Photo Fix > Adjust.**

Following a short time, your picture goes through some basic changes. These changes are the same as those that would be made if the Smart Photo Fix feature's proposed settings were accepted. If you don't like the changes you made to your picture, go to **Edit > Undo**. To make changes, select Adjust Smart Photo Fix and use the choices that appear. You can also try other choices in the Adjust menu, such as **Brightness and Contrast > Curves and Brightness and Contrast Levels**.

Adjust the fundamental flaws with the help of Smart Photo Fix

1. Click on **Adjust** and then on **Smart Photo Fix**. The original picture is shown in the Before pane at the top of the dialog box.
2. When you're done with any of the tasks, click OK.

You can also do the following:
- **Brighten or make the image darker:** To make the picture brighter or darker, type or set a value in the Overall, Shadows, and Highlights controls, or move the right sliders in the Brightness group box. **Note**: Setting a positive value makes the picture brighter while setting a negative value makes the picture darker.
- **Increase or reduce saturation:** To raise or lower the saturation, you can move the slider, change the type of saturation, enter a number in the saturation control, or raise or lower the saturation. Note that positive settings make colors look more vivid, while negative settings make them less vivid.
- **Sharpen the photo's edges:** To make the edges of the picture sharper, enter a number, choose a type, or move the slider in the Focus control.

If you pick **Suggest Settings or Reset to Default**, you can change all the settings back to their original state or values. If you check the box next to Advanced Options, the Smart Photo Fix feature's extra options will be used.

Use advanced options of the Smart Photo Fix

1. In the box for the Smart Photo Fix option, check the box next to Advanced Options.
2. When you're done with any of the jobs in the table below, click OK.

You can also do the following:
- **For balancing colors, use sample points:** You should look at the white balance. The black, gray, and white parts of the picture that are neutral are shown in the Before window. **Note**: No sample points can be found for some pictures because they don't have any black, gray, or white areas.
- **Ignore the sample points in the picture:** The box that says "White Balance" should be cleared. By checking the box again, the sampling points are brought back.
- **Add extra sampling points:** Click the areas that need to be black, gray, or white in the Before box.
- **Delete a sampling point:** To get rid of a sampling point, click on it in the before panes. Also, changes will be made to both the after and before panes.
- **Darken the photo's darkest pixels:** To make the photo's darkest pixels lighter, move the Black slider to the right or type a number into the box next to it.
- **Lighten the photo's palest pixels:** Move the White slider to the right or enter a number in the box next to the slider to make the photo's palest pixels lighter.

To keep white balance problems from happening, don't click on any color other than black, white, or gray while adding sample points. For example, don't click on an area that you know is blue. To make something black, white, or gray, just click on the area you want to change.

Sampling points cannot be moved or dragged

The histogram is only there to look nice; you can't move or change any of its parts. The original (Before) form of the picture is in the gray area, and the changes are shown in the red overlay area. When you move the black slider, the black triangle also moves. When you move the white slider, the white triangle also moves.

Brighten images

Lighting problems happen a lot in photos. Dark parts of photos taken in bright light often don't have enough clarity. If the background is too dark or there is too much difference between the light and dark parts of the picture, you can make the darker, underexposed parts of the picture brighter. You can change a color's brightness, which shows how pure or bright it is.

Bring out the best in your shot

1. Go to **Adjust** and then **Fill Flash**.
2. Type or add a number in the Strength slider (between 0 and 100) to tell it how much to brighten the darker items.

3. Enter a number or put a number into the Saturation control to change the whole image's color saturation. Saturation is increased by values larger than 0 and decreased by values greater than 0.
4. Click the OK button.

Note: If parts of a picture are both too light and too dark, go to **Adjust** > **Fill Flash** and then Adjust Backlighting.

Darken pictures

Sometimes, too much light in the background of a picture makes the whole thing invisible. The same thing happens when there is too much flash on the subject in a picture. It is possible to make the bright, overexposed parts of a picture darker.

Darken your picture

1. Go to Adjust and choose **Backlighting**.
2. If you want to change how dark the lighter parts are, move the Strength scale from 0 to 100.
3. To set the overall color saturation of the image, type a number into the Saturation control or set one. Saturation is increased by values larger than 0 and decreased by values greater than 0.
4. Click the OK button.

Note: If parts of a picture are both too light and too dark, go to **Adjust** > **Fill Flash** and then **Adjust** > **Backlighting**.

Eliminating the purple ruffles

Digital photos often have problems where parts of a color picture are overexposed and have purple cloud rings around them. This problem, called fringing, is often very clear when a bright sky appears in the background of a picture and a light purple circle forms around the edges of the subject of the picture. You can easily use PaintShop Pro to find this problem and fix it in your picture.

Take off the purple fringe that's on your picture

- Go to **Adjust** > **One Step Purple Fringe Fix**. After a short delay, your picture is changed instantly.

Removing digital noise

When talking about photos, "**noise**" means small bits of color that make the picture less clear. Usually, these specks are caused by the sensor on your digital camera being too small or by bad lighting. If you make a picture of a clear blue sky bigger, you can see little spots of orange, red, purple, green, and other colors. One Step Noise Removal, AI Denoise, and Digital Noise Removal are the three noise removal tools in PaintShop Pro that work well. When you use a noise reduction command, the software looks at your picture, finds the noise flaws, and fixes them while keeping the picture's important edge details.

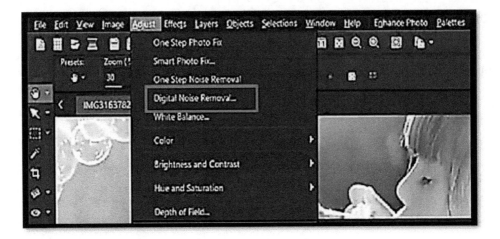

- **One-Step Noise Removal:** You can add noise reduction to your shot right away using the One Step Noise Removal command.
- **Artificial intelligence (AI) denoise**: AI can be used to look at the noise in the picture. If you choose "Enhanced," you can change how much noise is reduced.
- **Digital noise removal:** gives you more precise control over how the fixes are used.

Digital Noise Removing command

With the Digital Noise Removal command, you have more options for how to get rid of digital camera noise in your photos. Most of the time, the noise in pictures taken with the same camera shows up in the same places. Make a preset if you want to make the same changes to all of these photos.

In the following cases, using this command might be the best course of action:

- Using the command with low settings will help make the picture clearer without softening it too much for pictures that probably have a lot of noise, like a video whiteboard clip.
- You should only use this command on important parts of photos taken with the default settings that need to be fixed, like picture artifacts around the subject.
- You can choose which color groups to keep and which to discard in photos that have parts you don't want the noise reduction process to affect. One example is that you might choose not to change the skin tones in a picture. You can identify these safe areas as many times as you want.

Removing digital noise rapidly

- Click on **Adjust** and then **One-Step Noise Removal**. In the end, after a short pause, the noise turns off by itself.

44

Make use of AI Denoise to analyze and remove the noise

1. Start by going to **Adjust** > **AI Denoise**.
2. **Do one of these things:**
   - If you want a quick fix, choose Simple.
   - If you want a stronger fix, choose Enhanced and move the Strength scale to change how strong it is. If you know that using a GPU speeds up processing, you should check the box next to it.
   - Click "OK." There is a green progress bar at the bottom of the program window that you can use to see how the AI research is going.

Remove digital noise with the use of more complex solutions

1. Go to **Adjust** and select **Digital Noise Removal**. **Note**: The picture sample in the Remove Noise tabbed area has three crosshairs. There are noise samples in the bright, mid-tone, and dark parts of the picture that make up the markers. When you slide the box in front of the window, you can move the crosshair and change the sample area at the same time.
2. In the Remove Noise tab, check the box next to Link detail sizes to change the small, medium, and large settings relatively.
3. Type numbers into the **Small, Medium, and Large** settings. It is up to these choices to decide how much to fix small, medium, and large noise patterns.
4. Type or enter a number in the Correction Blend slider to choose how much the fixed picture will blend in with the new one. The levels of noise reduction range from 0.0 (no noise reduction) to 100.0 (full processing of the whole picture). 70 is the default.
5. Type or enter a number in the Sharpening control to decide how much, if any, sharpening should be done to the picture after the noise is gone. This number is set to 0 as default.
6. Click the OK button.

You can further:

- **Independently set light, mid-tone, and dark area adjustments:** Before you add a value for Small, Medium, or Large, uncheck the box next to Link detail sizes.
- **View details of the sample areas:** Click on a crosshair to get a better look at the area in the Before and After screens.
- **Add a crosshair for the sample area:** Just drag in the "Before" window.
- **Remove the crosshair for the sample area:** Drag one corner of an adjustment box to the opposite corner on the Before pane.

Ten sample zones are the most that can be used. A completely black or white area of the picture or the edge of the picture shouldn't be taken because it could lead to too much smoothing. Getting rid of moire patterns is not something that the Digital Noise Removal tool can do. Check the box next to Camera preset and click the Store Preset button to save the settings as a preset that is unique to the camera and picture. When the Camera preset checkbox is checked, the Load Preset drop-list only shows previously saved camera presets and not the usual presets. Do not select the Camera preset checkbox. To save the choices as a regular preset, click the Save Preset button. Select **Adjust > Add/Remove Noise > AI Artifact Removal** before running a noise removal command to get the best results when working with JPEG pictures.

Protect image areas from the noise corrections

1. Go to **Adjust** and select **Digital Noise Removal**.
2. Click on the **"Protect Image"** tab.
3. Use the Before pane to pan and zoom to see the area you want to defend.
4. Hold down Ctrl and move the mouse over the place you want to protect. When you hold down Ctrl in the picture window and look at the Remove Noise tab, there is no crosshair.
5. Type or set numbers in the Selected hue range group box's Hue and Range controls. The values as they are now are the same as the area that was sampled. You can change the color knob manually by moving it inside the ring.
6. Move any of the seven handles on the graphs in the Protect chosen hue range group box to the bottom to lessen the amount of smoothing and correction that is done to that hue range section. For example, if you drag just the middle graph handle to the bottom of the graph, you can turn off the mid-tone of that color range.
7. Click the OK button. If you choose "Reset Current," you can undo any changes you made to a certain range of colors. To undo all of your color changes, click **"Reset All."**

Remove chromatic aberrations from the image

When the camera takes a picture with the wrong colors, this is called chromatic aberration. Most of the time, a bad lens is to blame for chromatic aberration in film cameras.

Chromatic aberration in digital cameras may result from several reasons, such as the ones listed below:

- Sometimes, the camera's built-in lens aberration can make the edges of the picture look fuzzy. Digital cameras record light rays that are far from the optical axis. This means that pictures taken with telephoto and zoom lenses are more likely to have chromatic aberrations.
- This can happen because of the camera's auto-exposure mode, which tells the camera what exposure setting to use.
- Different parts of the sensor can pick up different colors, and these colors can come together to make one pixel. The process is called "demosaicing." After processing, the camera may do things like sharpness, noise reduction, and artifact removal.

Eliminate chromatic aberrations in photographs

1. Go to Adjust and choose **Chromatic Aberration Removal**.
2. Make sure you can see the Before and After panes at the top of the text box.
3. Make the size control in the dialog box at least 200% bigger. Above the zoom button are the **"Before" and "After"** panes. You can get a better look at the photo's trouble spots by

zooming in **200**%.

4. To make a picture area that can be seen in the Before pane, click the Pan button and move the image around.
5. In the Before box, drag to find the area that needs to be fixed. **Note**: The area that needs to be fixed is shown by the sample box. This can be done up to ten times. Each sample box is labeled as "**Sample n**" (where n is a number between 1 and 10 in the List of Samples area in the middle of the dialog box). The average color of the sampled area is shown by a color swatch to the left of each sample description.
6. Choose a sample entry from the List of Samples.
7. By typing a number or setting one in the Range control, you can find the color range of the active sample. This range affects the range of pixels that need to be fixed. The range you choose is shown in the color box right above the Range button.
8. To change the Radius control's value, type or enter a number to set the size of the sample aberration. Take note that 10 is the default number. The best numbers are usually those that are between 4 and 20. Values greater than 10 are helpful for sampling areas with sensor blooming errors. Values less than 10 help get rid of 1- or 2-pixel flaws caused by demosaicing or for working with pictures smaller than 1 megapixel. It is best to set the Radius control to the smallest number that fixes the aberration.
9. Click the **OK** button.

You can further do the following:

- **Resize a sample box:** Just moves the handle on the sample box.
- **Delete a sample box button:** After you choose a sample box, click Remove.
- **Remove the sample box:** To get rid of the sample box, Draw a line from one corner to the corner diagonally across from it. Stop when the two corners touch.
- **Show the image regions that are affected:** Check the box that says "Show Differences." In the After pane, the places that were affected are shown by white spots on black. Greater amounts of adjustment are shown by brighter areas.
- **Preview the outcome on the image:** The Preview on Image box should be checked, and the Show Differences box should also be checked.

After making the changes, run the effect again to get more than 10 sample boxes. By checking the box next to **Result on the New Layer**, you can make a new layer that will hold the fixed picture automatically. With this option, your original image is hidden on a separate layer. If you don't check this box, the changes will be made on the same layer as the original picture. You can cut down on the number of "**false corrections**" by first making a decision and then checking the Result on the New Layer box. This command can also be used on individual layers of a picture.

Using Lens Correction to fix distortion, vignetting, and chromatic aberration

If your pictures have problems with the lens, you can fix them with the choices under Lens Correction. Lens Correction can be applied to JPEG, TIFF, and RAW picture files.

Distortion

Some types of distortion can happen with fixed-focal length, or "**prime**," lenses. However, zoom lenses with a lot of different focal lengths have the most distortion. When you zoom in on a picture in a way that isn't even from the edges to the middle, you get barrel and pincushion distortion. The word "**barrel distortion**" refers to an image that looks rounded because the lens's magnification drops off at the edges. A pinched or squished look along the edges of a picture is called pincushion distortion. You can get rid of this distortion by looking at a group of photos taken with a lens at different focal lengths. Each lens has its own Barrel and Pincushion qualities. Inside Corel PaintShop Pro, there are sheets for more than one lens and camera combo.

Chromatic aberration

As light moves through a lens, it bends in different ways, which can cause another type of distortion called chromatic aberration, or CA distortion. Because of this, edges in high-contrast scenes, like tree branches against a bright sky, have a color shift that isn't smooth and a color fringe that often looks purple. When zoom lenses are used at their widest and longest focal lengths, they cause the most distortion. CA can be gotten rid of by changing the data for the colors that show the most distortion.

Vignetting

It can be caused by optics (the lens), the sensor (many sensors are less sensitive to light that comes at them from an angle), or something else, like a filter or lens hood that casts shadows on the edges of an image. Vignetting is when light falls off of the edges of an image and makes them darker. Vignetting can be fixed by making the edges of a picture brighter. To draw attention to the main subject, some photographers choose to use a vignette effect in their images. It is possible to add or remove vignetting with Lens Correction. When adding a vignette, the cropped area of the picture is always used. But when fixing a vignette, the whole original frame is used. You can use either the Automatic or Manual settings to fix things.

Using camera and lens profiles that are already built into PaintShop Pro, automatic corrections can be made to your images.

- To enable correction, turn Lens Correction on or off.
- Automatic cropping makes the image bigger to fit the image frame.
- **Manufacturer drop-list:** if a picture has information in it, it will show the camera

manufacturer immediately. If not, you can set it yourself.

- **Model drop-list:** this lets you choose the camera model manually or automatically if the picture has information in it.
- **Lens drop-list:** Shows the lens that was used to take the picture automatically (if the image has metadata). **Note**: Based on the data it has access to, the software will sometimes choose the best match. By picking the right camera model, brand, and lens from the lists, you can fix the wrong figures. These say which shape should be used to get rid of distortion.
- **Focal Length:** If a picture has information in it, it will show you the focal length setting that the lens was on when it was taken, or you can change it manually.

You can choose your correction settings instead of using factors from application-built profiles when you use manual. This is good for lenses that aren't in the lens correction database yet.

The following controls are part of the correction for chromatic aberration:

- **R/C**: controls color shift along the Red/Cyan color line.
- **B/Y:** This factor controls how colors change along the Blue/Yellow color line.

The following is included in the vignette correction:

- This setting lets you turn vignette correction on or off. These controls don't work with any other types of lens correction.
- **Strength:** The strength of a correction tells you how bright (positive or right) or dark (negative or left) it will be.
- **Radius:** This number tells the adjustment how far into the picture it should go.

Use Lens Correction

1. **Take one of the following actions:**
   - Open the image in the Camera RAW Lab to get to the Lens tab for RAW shots.
   - Click **Adjust** to fix the lens on JPEG and TIFF pictures.
2. After you choose **Automatic or Manual**, you can change the settings as needed.

Adjusting distortions caused by the lens

Photos can be skewed because of the lenses on cameras. These distortions are most noticeable in wide-angle photos, close-up photos with set focal lengths, and photos taken with cheap lenses (like disposable cameras).

Note: If you're going to crop a picture, you should fix the lens distortion first.

The many types of lens distortion

These three types of lens distortion can make straight lines look wavy, and PaintShop Pro can fix them:
- **Barrel distortion:** There is barrel distortion, which makes the image's center look like it's being pushed out. If you want to change the distortion, the axis of the camera lens needs to meet up with the middle of the picture.
- **Fisheye distortion:** The image looks like it was blown up like a balloon or stuck on top of a sphere, which is called fisheye distortion. The edges of the picture look messed up.
- **Pincushion distortion:** When the image's center seems pushed in, this is called pincushion distortion.

Here are the steps to fix barrel distortion:
1. Click on Adjust and then on **Barrel Distortion Correction**.
2. If there are any curved lines in the picture, enter the right number for the Strength control to make them straight.
3. Click "**OK**."

If you check the Preserve central scale box, you can change the scale in the middle of the image by adding or taking away pixels. The Result Size group box shows changes made to the width and height of the source image.

Adjusting for the fish-eye distortion

1. In the Adjust menu, choose **Fisheye Distortion Correction**.
2. Enter or change the Field of View control to the right number to get rid of the distortion.
3. Click "**OK**."

Note: If you check the "Preserve central scale" box, you can change the scale in the middle of the image by adding or taking away pixels. The Result Size group box shows changes made to the width and height of the source image.

Adjust the distortion of the pincushion

1. Under Adjust, click on **Pincushion Distortion Correction**.
2. If you see any crooked lines in the picture, type or set a number in the Strength control until the lines are straight.
3. Click "OK."

CHAPTER 5
WORK WITH GRADIENTS

A gradient is when two or more colors blend into each other over time. You can paint, draw, or fill an area with gradients to make effects or color changes that stand out. You can use gradients to give things depth, make Web buttons with shadows and highlights, and make things look shiny or bright. Grainy lines that go from black to white can be used as masks, and they can also be used to blend images on a Web page into other material.

Applying your current gradient

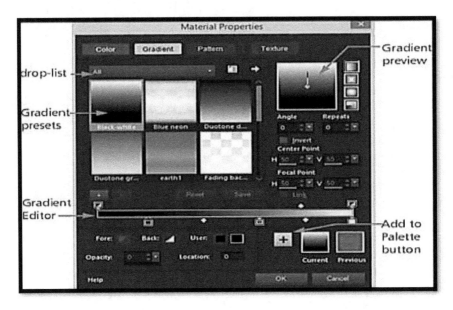

From the Style drop-down menu on the Materials panel, pick either the Foreground and Stroke Properties box or the Background and Fill Properties box. Then click the Gradient button. The gradient that was most recently chosen is used.

To pick gradients

1. **In the Materials menu, pick one of the following options:**
   - Find the Foreground and Stroke Properties box and click on it to pick a foreground gradient.
   - Find the Background and Fill Properties box and click on it to pick a background color.
2. Press and hold the Gradient button.
3. If you need to, use the group drop-list to pick a group for the gradients you want.
4. Click on a thumbnail of a gradient.

5. **Pick one of the options below:**
   - **Style:** This option lets you pick a color that is straight, rectangular, sunburst-shaped, or radial.
   - **Angle:** Sets the angle or direction of the gradient, which can be anywhere from 0 to 359 degrees. This setting can only be used for gradients that are linear, rectangular, or radial.
   - **Repeats**: This option tells the gradient pattern how many times it will repeat (from 0 to 999).
   - **Invert**: Invert changes the gradient's colors from one to the other.
   - **Center Point:** This option finds the point where the gradient starts and gives you its horizontal and vertical coordinates. A fraction of the width of the fill space is used to show the distance. If the gradient's nucleus is not in the middle of the item, you can change the gradient's center point to fill in rings and other shapes. With this choice, you can only use circular, sunburst, or rectangular gradients.
   - **Focal Place:** This property sets the point where the gradient's foreground color begins in terms of both time and space. A fraction of the width of the fill space is used to show the distance. By moving the focus point, you can fill in circles and other shapes where the light source isn't in the middle. This choice can only be used when the Link check box is not checked. It only works with rectangular and sunburst gradients.
   - **Link center and focus points:** You can link the center and focus points to get the same number for both. Uncheck the box to change the focus point without changing the center point. With this choice, you can only use sunburst and rectangular colors.
6. Click the OK button.

You can further do the following:

- **Save a gradient as a swatch that you can view later:** Click the button that says "Add to Palette."
- **Apply the most recent information to all tools:** Choose All tools from the materials menu. Then, if you uncheck the box, the current elements will be used on the current tool.

You can also change the center point with the control needle or markers that show up in the preview of the gradient. In case the Link check box is not checked, you can move the focus point by dragging the crosshairs on the gradient.

Saving edited gradients

1. On the Gradient page, click "Save."
2. Give the gradient a name and then click OK.

Create gradients

1. On the Gradient page, click the New Gradient button.

2. Name the new gradient and then click OK. To make the gradient, two markers with the unique color are put at 0% and 100%.

Rename gradients

1. Click the "More Options" button on the Gradient page and choose **"Resource Manager."**
2. Click on the color you want to change the name of in the Resource Manager box.
3. Type a name into the Rename Resource box, and then click OK.

Erase gradients

1. Pick a gradient that you made on the Gradient page.
2. Choose **"Delete Gradient"** from the list.
3. When asked if you want to delete the file, click "Yes."

To Edit Gradients

You can change a gradient's colors, where it changes colors, and how transparent it is. You can change patterns that are already there, or you can make your own. You can also save, remove, and change the name of a gradient. **Markers and midpoints on the Gradient Editor show the colors, transition points, and transparency of a gradient:**

- **Markers:** At the top of the color bar are markers that show how transparent something is. There are colored marks below the gradient bar.
- **Midpoints:** These are the spots where two colors mix evenly or where the transparency is 50%. There is a point in the middle that can be found anywhere between any two marks.

You can add and remove markers and change their color, position, and how transparent they are. **Note:** When you edit and save a default gradient, the changes are final. To keep the basic gradients, save your changes to a new gradient file.

Relocating either the midpoints or the markers

- Move the marking or middle point to a different spot in the Gradient Editor. You can also type a number into the Location box after hitting the marker or in the middle of selecting it.

Add markers

To put a marker, click on a spot on the Gradient Editor. For a color marker, click under the gradient bar. For a transparency marker, click above the gradient bar. The Fore, Back, or Custom color of the gradient bar, which is what is underlined right now, is used to make the marker.

Erase markers

When you drag markers away from the gradient bar in the gradient editor, you can get rid of them.

Altering the color of a marker

1. In the Gradient Editor, click below the gradient bar to pick a marker. The triangle at the top of the marking goes from white to black.
2. **When you're done with one of these tasks, click OK:**
   - **To utilize the foreground color:** Pick "Fore" from the list.
   - To change the background color, press the "Back" button.
   - **To utilize the currently defined custom color:** Click on the user button.
   - **To select a new custom color:** Pick a color from the page by clicking on the swatch next to the "User" button.
   - **To choose a color directly from the gradient itself:** Pick the gradient bar.

As you apply the next gradient that has those colors, the picture's foreground and background colors are used. This is because gradient colors change over time. To make a gradient that always has the same colors, give all of the markers unique colors from the User swatch. This is called "static gradient colors."

Relocating either the midpoints or the markers

1. To pick it, click the marker above the gradient bar in the gradient editor.
2. Here is where you type or set a number for opacity. The numbers range from 0% (no transparency) to 100% (opaque). At 100%, the pixels below are completely hidden.

Edit all gradients applied to vector objects and see modifications in real time

1. First, click the Pick tool on the Tools bar. Next, in the image window, pick a vector object that has a gradient added to it.
2. To open the Material Properties box, click the swatch in the Materials panel that says Background and Fill Properties.
3. Click the Gradient tab and change any of the gradient settings.

Export and Import Gradients

As you work on a new gradient, you might want to share it so that you can use it in another program. These gradients are saved in a GRD file format, which is used by many other apps. You can also import gradients that are saved as GRD files.

To export gradients

1. On the Gradient page, pick the gradient you want to export.
2. Go to "More Options" and choose "Export."
3. Pick a place to save the gradient. The usual gradients are in the Gradients folder in the Paint Shop Pro software folder.
4. In the File name box, give the new gradient a name.

5. Click "Save."

Importing GRD gradients

1. Go to the Gradient page and choose Import from the menu that says "More Options."
2. Find the folder that has the gradient you want to add. There is a list of all the GRD files in the folder.
3. Choose the filename for the gradient and then click "Open."

Apply Transparency or Color Gradient via the Gradient fill tool

With the Gradient Fill tool, you can add a gradient to the canvas, a selection, or a shape while you work with them. You can change the colors, gradation, transparency, and direction right in the picture window. By default, the Gradient Fill tool uses the most recent gradient that was picked on the **Material Properties** > **Gradient page** and changes it based on the choices made in the Tool Options menu at the time. You can change how transparent a color gradient is generally by adding a new layer and changing how transparent that layer is. The level of transparency for each node can be changed (opacity stops).

Apply your color gradients using the Gradient Fill tool

1. Choose the Gradient Fill tool from the Tools menu. It is in a group with the Flood Fill tool in a flyout.
2. To put the gradient line in the right place, drag an item, a pick, or the canvas across the picture window.

Note: The Gradient page of the Material Properties dialog box always uses the most recent foreground gradient that was picked. If you right-click and drag, the most recent color chosen for the background swatch will be used.

3. **To change the color of the gradient, do any of these things:**
   - Click and drag the rotating lever to change the angle of the gradient.
   - To add color, drag a color swatch from the Materials menu onto the line of the gradient.
   - To get rid of a color, drag a swatch away from the gradient line.
   - To change a color, select a swatch on the gradient line by clicking it (a blue outline will show that you have selected it). Next, either click the Color Picker icon in the Tool Options window and choose a new color, or from the Materials menu, drag a different color swatch to the selected swatch.
   - To change how the colors blend, drag the color swatches along the length of the gradient line.
   - Change the settings in the Tool Options panel to change the type of gradient or flip the gradient.
4. **In the Tool Options panel, check the Opacity stop box to change the gradient's transparency. Then, do one of the options below:**

- If you want to change the Opacity setting in the Tool Options menu, click on an opacity stop on the gradient line.
- To add an opacity stop to a gradient line, click it.
- To remove an opacity stop, drag the node you want to remove from the gradient line.
- Click and drag the node along the gradient line to change how the stops in the opacity change.

5. To get back to changing color swatches, check the Color stop box in the Tool Options group. Before you use the gradient fill, you can make a new layer in the Layers panel and adjust the Opacity scale to the right level to change how transparent the gradient fill is overall.

CHAPTER 6
ADJUST IMAGES

When you look at your photos in PaintShop Pro, you can see problems that you need to fix. There are clear flaws in some pictures, like when the subject is too dark. You might be able to tell that other pictures need work but not know what to do about it. You can change pictures in PaintShop Pro by hand or let the program do the basic editing for you.

Fix frequent issues

PaintShop Pro has a lot of quick and useful commands and tools that can help you fix some common shooting problems. Some correction directions open a dialog box with options that can be used to change the correction.

If you want to crop or resize the image, you should do it first before using a fix. The below contains a problem and the best way to solve it from the Edit tab.

- **The image should seem better overall:** If you choose **Adjust One Step Photo Fix**, some basic photo fixes will be done automatically. If you want to make some basic changes to your photos, select **Adjust Smart Photo Fix**.
- **The picture has some too-dark areas (underexposed):** Select **Adjust Fill Flash or Adjust Brightness and Contrast Fill Light/Clarity** to quickly fix the dark parts of a picture. If you choose **Adjust Smart Photo Fix**, all of the changes will be made. If you choose Adjust Brightness and Contrast, you'll see steps on how to change the brightness and contrast. You should try the Curves and Levels directions the most.
- **The picture has some too-light areas (overexposed):** To quickly change a photo's bright spots, choose Modify Backlighting. If you choose Adjust Smart Photo Fix, all of the changes will be made. If you choose **Adjust Brightness and Contrast**, you'll see steps on how to change the brightness and contrast. You should try the Curves and Levels directions the most.
- **The image has a specific area that is either too dark or too light:** When you use a selection tool, be careful to only pick out the part of the picture that is too bright or too dark. **Note**: The One Step Photo Fix and Smart Photo Fix functions work on the whole picture, even if you've already chosen something.
- **The contrast in the image is either too low or too high:** If you want to change the brightness or other settings, select **Adjust Smart Photo Fix**. You can also go to **Brightness and Contrast > Adjust > Brightness/Contrast**.
- **Someone in the picture seems to have strange skin tones:** If you want to fix this, go to **Adjust > White Balance**.
- **Purple fringe and other color aberrations are seen on the edges in images:** Selecting **Adjust > One Step Purple Fringe Fix** will get rid of this for you. To use the advanced settings for fixing chromatic aberration, choose **Adjust Chromatic Aberration Removal**.

- **An individual in the image has a red eye:** To quickly get rid of red eyes, select the Red Eye tool. Choose **Adjust Red Eye Removal** to use the more advanced choices for getting rid of red eyes.
- **Someone in the picture has discolored skin, unpolished teeth, or imperfections on their skin:** From the Tools bar, choose the Makeover tool. In the Tool Options box, change the mode to Toothbrush, Blemish Fixer, or Suntan.
- **The image seems hazy or foggy:** To fix a bad exposure, choose **Adjust Brightness and Contrast Levels**. To improve clarity, choose **Adjust Brightness and Contrast Local Tone Mapping.**
- **The image doesn't seem to be crisp:** To do high-frequency sharpness, use **Adjust Sharpness High Pass Sharpen.** Choose **Adjust Sharpness** and a command to use more sharpening methods.
- **The image needs to be straightened:** From the Tools menu, choose the Straighten tool.
- **The perspective of the things in the picture seems off:** Pick out the Perspective Correction tool from the toolbar.

Rotate image

If you rotate a picture by 90 degrees (vertically), you can change its orientation to either portrait or landscape. If your camera has features that can tell when a picture was taken in portrait mode, it will automatically turn it to the right position. You can also move a picture on the canvas or by setting a degree of rotation that lets you turn it anyway. Another thing you can do from the Manage menu is rotate JPEG files without losing any of the picture data.

To rotate an image

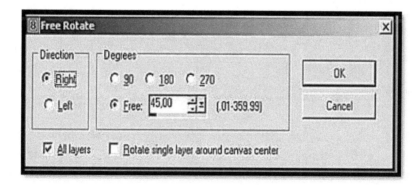

Choose a picture, and then carry out one of the tasks listed below:

- **Rotate 90 degrees clockwise or counterclockwise:** You can choose to rotate the picture left or right.
- **Rotate a picture at a certain angle:** Click on Free Rotate under Image selection. Pick either the Right or the Left option in the Free Rotate dialog box to decide which way the thing

will rotate. In the Degrees group box, choose the "Free" option. Then, enter or change a value in the control.

- **Rotate an image interactively:** From the Tools bar, choose the Pick tool. To turn the picture, drag the rotation lever, which is the square with a line going through it to the rotation pivot point. The cursor changes into two curved lines when it is above the rotation handle.

You can also rotate a picture by pressing the Rotate Right or Rotate Left buttons on the Standard toolbar menu. Moving the circle in the middle of the picture, which is the rotation pivot point, while holding down Ctrl will let you change the center of rotation before you rotate the image dynamically.

Reduce the size of photographs

To make layouts better or draw attention to a different part of the picture, unwanted parts of an image may be cut off. PaintShop Pro helps with cropping by having settings for common picture ratios like 1:1, 2:3, 3:4, and 16:9.

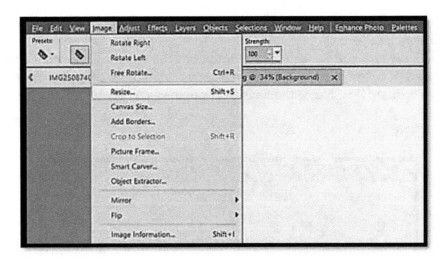

Cropping a picture makes it smaller, so it takes up less room on your hard drive. Cropping can also improve color changes by getting rid of color areas that aren't being used. If a picture needs to be trimmed and its colors changed, crop it first and then change the colors. Before you print, you can crop a picture to fit a certain size. There is also the option to pick out a part of the picture and crop it to the edges of that part. You can also make a new picture from the cropped area. You can rotate a picture around the crop rectangle to make it straight or give it an artistic angle. You can crop a picture by choosing which parts of it are opaque (not see-through). This way of cropping is helpful when you want to get rid of see-through parts at the edges of the picture. You can also use the crop area to cover the opaque part of a single layer or the whole picture.

Composition guides

You can use composition rules to make your composition even stronger when you crop. A regular grid, the Rule of Thirds, the Golden Spiral, the Golden Ratio, the diagonal, and the triangle can all help you put together a picture.

Improve picture editing options

The Floating Crop toolbar allows you to instantly apply the following picture improvement options:

- Simple Photo Fix
- The depth of field is crucial

When you crop, the part of the picture that is outside the crop box is erased forever. You can save the edited version of your picture with a different name by pressing "Save As." The original photo will stay the same.

Crop image

1. Choose the **Crop tool** from the list of tools in the toolbar.

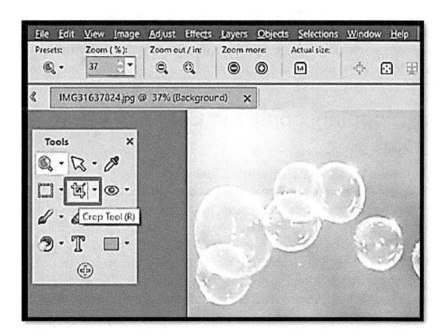

2. You can change the size of the crop area by moving any of the handles or edges. To move the crop box, put the cursor inside it and drag it. You can use a fixed crop size by choosing it from the Presets drop-list on the Crop tool's floating toolbar or from the drop-list on

the Tool Options palette. To use a composition guide, click the **Composition Guide** button on the floating menu. This turns the guide on and off, and then you can pick a guide from a list.

3. When you're ready to crop the picture, click the **Apply** button on the Tool Options palette or the floating toolbar for the **Crop** tool.

You can further accomplish the following:

- **Apply the crop by utilizing your keyboard or mouse:** To crop, just double-click or press Enter in the crop box.
- **Size the size of the crop rectangle on the Tool Options palette:** You should use the height and width settings to set the pixel sizes.
- **Constrain the crop area to its present proportions**: Check the box next to Maintain aspect ratio on the Tool Options screen. You can only crop rectangles that have certain customization choices.
- **The crop rectangle should be 90 degrees rotated:** Pick **Rotate Crop Rectangle** from the toolbar that floats above.
- **Rotate the picture by a certain amount about the crop rectangle:** Turn the picture around the crop box in any way you want.

After you crop a picture, you may notice that the Tool Options palette's Width and Height values are both set to 0.100. These settings don't show the cropped picture size. If you want to see the image's measurements after cropping, go to **Image > Image Information.** When the picture is turned, the crop rectangle might go past the edges of it. When you work on a certain layer, the area outside the original picture will either be clear or filled with the background. There's Magic Fill that can help you fill in these gaps.

During cropping, apply the Enhance Photo choices to the photos

1. Choose the **Crop tool** from the list of tools.
2. **Do any of these things before you crop the picture:**
   - To turn on or off **One Step Photo Fix**, click the icon that goes with it.
   - To turn on or off **Depth of Field**, click the icon that goes with it. If you click and hold the button, a grid will appear. Click the part of the grid that you want to keep in focus, and then use the Blur and Size sliders to make that part of the grid in focus.
3. Drag on the image to set the crop area. You can use any other crop choices you want.
4. When you're ready to crop the picture, hit the **Apply** button on the Crop tool's floating toolbar to pick it.

Crop images for printing

1. Choose the Crop tool from the list of tools in the toolbar.
2. Next, outline the crop area by moving it around inside the picture.

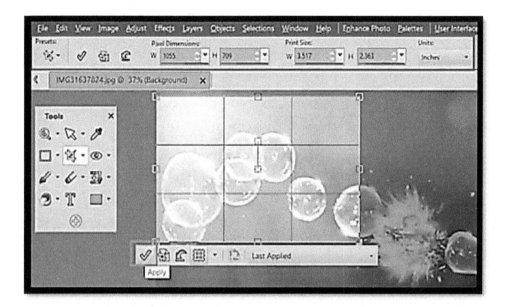

3. In the Tool options palette, open the box that says "Specify print size." Check it out. Keep in mind that if the selected print size box is checked, the picture resolution will change whenever you change the document size or pixel dimensions' height and width controls. The current resolution will also be shown in the upper right part of the unit's drop list.

4. Pick inches or centimeters from the unit drop list. Please keep in mind that the pixels option is not available for this cropping option.

5. Use the height and width controls to set or enter the size numbers. After that, the crop area is made the size you want it to be, and the picture quality can be raised or lowered as needed.

6. Click on the Apply button in the palette of tool options.

Crop to selection on an image

1. Pick out a part of the picture.

2. Click on **Image** and then **Crop to Selection**. For this option, you can use any kind of form. In PaintShop Pro, a crop area rectangle is put around choices that have odd shapes. When you crop to a feathered selection, the current background color fills in the feathered part of the selection. The Current Selection box in the Snap crop rectangle to group on the Tool Options menu can be checked with the Crop tool to crop to the current selection. Pick the place you want to crop, then press "**Apply**."

Crop to the opaque area in an image or layer

1. Choose the cropping tool.
2. **In the Tool Options menu, find the Snap Crop Rectangle To group box and pick one of the choices below:**
   - **Layer Opaque:** Picks out opaque parts of the current layer.

- **Merged Opaque:** Picks the opaque parts of all layers.
3. Change the area for the crop.
4. Click the **Apply** button on the Tool Options palette or the moving toolbar for the Crop tool. If the background of a layer is a solid color that doesn't show through, the crop area is the whole layer or picture.

Note: Parts that were opaque but not rectangular can still be see-through after cropping.

How to create a new image by cropping

1. Choose the Crop tool from the list of tools in the toolbar.
2. To set the crop area, drag a part of the picture.
3. Click the button in the Tool Options palette or on the Crop tool's floating toolbar to choose the Crop as a new picture option. The edited picture is still the one that is being used, even though a new picture has been made.

When you scan several photos together, this feature makes it easy to make new pictures. If you take four pictures at once, for example, you can quickly split each one into a separate file using this feature.

Bringing things into focus

Straightening photos is easy if you line up a straightening bar with a picture feature. PaintShop Pro turns the picture so that this adjusting bar is the right length and width. This feature is very helpful when a picture has a strong vertical or horizontal element, like a building or the sky.

Straighten image

1. Choose the Straighten tool from the list of tools in the toolbar.
2. To make a certain part of the picture straight, drag each straightening bar handle into place.

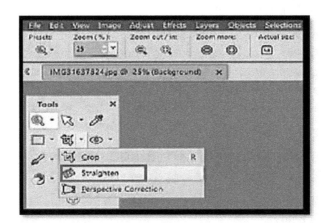

3. Choose one of these options from the drop-down menu next to Mode on the Tool Options palette: When the bar for straightening is in the vertical position, the picture is straightened by itself. The picture is turned around when the straightening bar is in the horizontal position.

4. Choose "**Apply**" from the list. One more option is to only straighten one layer. Before you choose the Straighten tool in the Layers box, click on the name of the layer.

You can further do the following:

- **Straighten a single layer:** On the layer's palette, choose the name of the layer before you choose the straighten tool.
- **Straighten the entire layers in the picture**: To rotate all layers, just check the box next to it on the tool's options palette.
- **Select a specific angle for the straightening bar:** In the tool's options palette, enter or set a value in the angle control.
- **Crop or mark the edges of the picture to make it rectangular after straightening:** On the tool's options palette, just check the box next to Crop Image.
- **Fill the edge areas of your picture with the background color:** Just unmark or uncheck the box next to "crop picture" on the tool's options palette.

CHAPTER 7
ADJUST WHITE BALANCE

Changing the colors of a picture can often make it look much better. Various lighting situations, cameras, and camera processing can all contribute to inaccurate coloration in images. Things that have been scanned might have strange color casts. PaintShop Pro has many color-balancing tools that can be used to make colors look natural and get rid of any color casts in your picture.

By following the steps for either a selection or the whole image, you can do the following:

- Make the colors in a picture look even without making it less bright.
- Change the red, blue, or green color of the given channel by a certain amount.
- Make photos that are fading more colorful and clearer.
- To make a photographic negative, change each pixel's color to the opposite of what it normally is. For example, change blue to yellow, black to white, yellow to blue, and white to black, and so on.
- To change the general color of your picture, you can change how much red, green, and blue it has.

Adjusting the White Balance

1. Click on **White Balance** under "**Adjust**."
2. Check the box next to Smart White Balance. That way, PaintShop Pro can look at the picture and make small changes on its own.
3. For warmer colors, move the temperature scale to the right. For cooler colors (bluer) (more orange), move it to the left.
4. Click "**OK**."

If you check the box next to "Advanced Options" and enter or change the temperature values in the Temperature and Tint controls in the White Balance group box, you can set correct tonal balance values; you can only do that if you know what the image's ideal color temperature is. The colors can be changed by changing the settings in the Enhance White Balance group box for Temperature and Tint.

Mix color channels

1. Under Adjust Color, choose **Channel Mixer**.
2. **Pick one of these things to do:**
   - Pick a color channel from the drop-down menu next to "Output channel" to change or keep the color picture.
   - Check the **Monochrome** box to change the picture to monochrome. Monochrome looks like sepia but has 16 million colors. The drop-list for the Output channel is gray.
3. The red, green, and blue controls in the Source Channels group box can be typed or set

to numbers, or the sliders can be moved to change the amount of each color in the channel. Changing the red channel and setting the red control to 50%, for example, cuts the amount of red in the picture to half of what it was before.

4. Adjust the slider for Constant. The scale starts at a value of 0. The color channel will get darker if you move the scale to the left. To make the color channel brighter, move the bar to the right.

5. Click "**OK**."

Restore the colors that have faded

1. Pick the choice that says "**Adjust Color Fade Correction.**" In the Before pane, drag to put the center of an image's important part (like a face).

2. In the "**Amount of corrective control**" area, change the value until the picture looks as real as it can. 45 is the default value. To get a good fix, use the lowest number possible. Too many changes can mix things, and areas of light and shadow may lose their definition.

3. Click "OK."

Produce the negative for the picture

- Go to **Image** and choose **Negative Image**.

Modify the color cast

1. Under **Adjust Color**, pick Red, Green, or Blue.

2. To change the amount of each color, type or set a number in the red, green, and blue settings. When the number is 0, the old value is kept. Use a good number to make more color appear. To remove some of the color, use a negative number. The image is tinted yellow, magenta, or cyan depending on how much blue is added to the picture.

3. Click "OK."

Make necessary adjustments to the contrast, brightness, and clarity

With PaintShop Pro, you can change how clear, dark, and bright your photos are. A contrast is the difference between the pixels that are brightest and darkest in a picture. With clarity, you can change the amount of information in a picture by looking at the contrast in certain areas.

You can perform the following by applying the instructions to a selection or a full image:

- Change the color and contrast manually
- Make your picture look clear and sharp to draw attention to the subject.
- Change each number of the brightness in your picture.
- Change the shadows, mid-tones, and highlights to make the changes in tone look smooth.
- Fixed the exposure
- Better even out the lightness values of the pixels across the range of brightness, from black to white
- If the full range of brightness isn't shown in the histogram, increase the total contrast.

- Change the image's gamma, contrast, and brightness.
- Make a picture that is only black and white.

Histograms

With a histogram, you can see a picture's tonal range and change how the highlights, mid-tones, and shadows are spread out. In other words, the histogram can tell you whether or not your image has been properly exposed, whether it is overexposed, underexposed, or both. Most digital cameras have an LCD screen that shows a histogram. Some cameras even let you change the scene's histogram before you take the picture. There are some tasks in PaintShop Pro that show the histogram in the text box. Some of these choices are Curves, Levels, the advanced mode of Smart Photo Fix, and Histogram Adjustment. **When examining a histogram, take note of the following:**

- The part of the image is black or almost black is shown on the left side of the histogram.
- The right side of the histogram displays the amount of images that are white or almost white.

In the Histogram Adjustment dialog box, the number of pixels is shown on the line for each value of the chosen channel. On the vertical line, which goes from 0 to 1, there are the most pixels in the graph. The horizontal axis shows the value of the channel that was picked. This value can be anywhere from 0 to 255. You can always see a picture's Histogram by going to **View** > **Palettes** > **Histogram**.

Adjust either the contrast or the brightness

1. To change the brightness and contrast, go to **Brightness and Contrast > Adjust > Brightness/Contrast**.

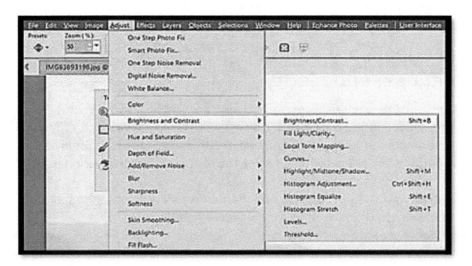

2. To change the brightness, type a letter or number. An image looks lighter when the number is positive and darker when the number is negative. Zero doesn't change anything

about the setting.

3. To change the contrast, enter a number or type it in. For comparison, a positive number makes it stronger, and a negative number makes it weaker. Zero doesn't change anything about the setting.

4. Click "**OK.**" Use the zoom control in the window box to change how the picture looks in the "**Before**" and "**After**" panes.

Bright up the dark areas and then work on the clarity

1. Click on **Adjust Brightness and Contrast** and then on **Fill Light/Clarity**.

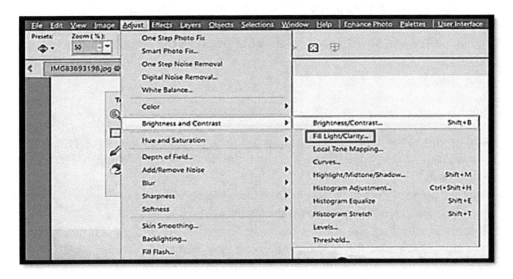

2. Fill Light lets you enter a number or write words. As the number goes up, the darkest parts of the image get lighter, and as the number goes down, it stays the same.

3. To change the Clarity, type a letter or enter a number. A positive number makes more details stand out, while a negative number makes things clearer. Zero doesn't change anything about the setting.

4. Click "**OK.**"

Improving both the depth and the clarity

1. Select **Local Tone mapping** from the list of Brightness and Contrast options.

2. Enter a number or type it into the Strength box. The smallest amount that will still work is what you should use. When the values are too high, unwanted artifacts show up in the image.

3. Click "OK." Use the zoom control in the window box to change how the picture looks in the "Before" and "After" panes.

How to adjust the brightness of the color channels

1. Click on **Curves** under Adjust Brightness and Contrast.
2. **Pick one of the color channels from the Channel drop-down menu:**
   - **RGB** lets you change the red, green, and blue channels of a composite histogram.
   - **Red**—you can only change the red channel.
   - **Green**—you can only change the green channel.
   - **Blue**: This button only lets you change the blue channel.
3. You can move the points on the graph to change how closely the input levels (the brightness of the original pixels) match the output levels (the brightness of the corrected pixels). As you move the point on the histogram, the old and new values for pixel lightness for each curve point are shown in the top left corner. This is the original value, which is shown on the left. The changed value, which is called the output value, is shown on the right.
4. Click "OK."

You can further:

- **Add a point to the curve:** To add a point to the curve, click on the spot on the curve where you want to put the point. **Note**: You can finetune the shape of the curve by adding more points to it.
- **Drag the point of the graph to remove it from the curve:** To move the current curve point more precisely, press or hold down the Arrow keys.
- **Automatically adjust the photo's contrast:** To change the photo's contrast automatically, click the Contrast button in the Auto group box. **Note**: Click this button if you like the colors of the picture but want to make the contrast stronger.
- **Automatically adjust or change the photo's white balance:** Find the Auto group box and click the Color button. This will change the photo's white balance automatically. **Note**: If you press this button, the photo's black and white points will be found immediately.
- **Automatically change the color and the contrast:** To make the color and contrast change on their own, click the Levels button in the Auto group box.
- **Set your own black, gray, or white point and then insert the dropper in one of those colors:** Choose your own black, gray, or white point, and then place the dropper in one of those colors. To do this, check the Dropper Color box. Pick out an area in the Before pane that you are sure is black, gray, or white, and then click on it. It changes the After pane and the image window if the Preview on Image setting is chosen.
- **Automatically choose the proper black, gray, or white point:** Place the mouse in the Before pane while holding down Alt. It will be possible to use the right color dropper while moving the mouse over medium, light, and dark areas.
- **Set the Auto Contrast, Color, and Levels buttons' histogram clipping parameters:** To change the histogram clipping settings for the Auto Contrast, Color, and Levels buttons, go to the menu and choose Options. You can set the Auto Color settings in the Auto Color Options dialog box for the Lower Limit, Upper Limit, and Strength controls to percentage

values. It's important to note that higher values for the Lower Limit and Upper Limit controls make the automatic settings more stable, while lower values make the automatic settings less risky. Lowering the Strength setting makes the clipping less noticeable.

- **Choose histogram clipping limits for the auto contrast, levels, and color buttons:** Click the Options button to set the histogram cutting limits for the auto contrast, levels, and color buttons. When you're in the auto color choices box, pick the percentage values for the strength control, the lower limit control, and the upper limit control. **Note**: The upper and lower limit controls make the automatic settings stronger or weaker. Higher values make the automatic settings stronger, and lower values make them weaker. Also, clipping is less noticeable when the strength number is low.
- **Reset all modified values to the original values:** To return all changed values to their previous states, press the "Reset" button next to the color dropper. You can also click the "Reset to Default" button, which is next to the "Save Preset" button.

Note: You can also use the zoom button in the dialog box to pick the view of the image you want to see in the Before and After panes.

Adjust the picture's mid-tones, highlights, and shadows

1. Go to **Adjust > Brightness and Contrast** and choose **Highlight**, **Midtone**, or **Shadow**.
2. **Pick one of the options below:**
   - When you use the absolute correction method, the 25% histogram point (Shadows), the 50% histogram point (Midtones), and the 75% histogram point are put exactly where they belong (Highlights). Depending on the picture, the Shadow, Midtone, and Highlight numbers are usually around 35, 50, and 65. As the number goes up or down, the area gets lighter or darker.
   - Relative adjustment method: The levels of lightness are different from how they were at the start. The area is lighter when the value is positive, and darker when the value is negative.
3. Type your values in the Shadow, Midtone, and Highlight controls.
4. Click the OK button.

Note: Use the zoom control in the text box to change how the picture looks in the Before and After panes.

Correct exposure by making use of histograms

1. Go to **Adjust > Brightness and Contrast** and choose **Histogram Adjustment**.
2. In the Edit group box, choose one of the options below:
   - **Luminance** lets you change the brightness of an image to get the right contrast.
   - **Colors** let you pick a color channel that you can change. If you click on Colors, you have to pick a color from the drop-down menu.

3. For Load Preset, choose **Default** from the drop-down menu. The picture doesn't change at all with the usual settings.

4. Adjust the Low slider. Look for a space on the left side of the histogram between the edge on the left and the graph's highest point. The fact that there is no gap shows that the image's darkest cells are not all black. Move the Low slider (the black triangle) until the line starts to rise. From 0 to 254, the Low control shows that the setting is low. In the bottom control, it shows the percentage of pixels between 0 and the low number. These pixels will lose their contrast. As a general rule, keep the Low number below 0.1%.

5. Adjust the High slider. Look for a space between the edge of the right window and the point on the right side of the histogram where the graph gets smaller and smaller until it stops. If there is a gap in the line, move the High slider (the white triangle) to it. After this is done, the image's lightest dots turn white. As a general rule, keep the High number below 0.1%.

6. Move the Gamma slider. If the image is too dark or too light, you should change the gamma value, which shows how the contrast has changed. To make the picture brighter, raise the gamma by one. Move the gray Gamma tool to the right. It looks like a triangle. The image can be made darker by moving the Gamma slider to the left.

7. Adjust the Midtones slider. If the curve has high points on the left and right sides and low points in the middle, the midtones need to be squished together. The shadows and highlights need to be made bigger so that you can see the information that is hidden in them. When taken against a dark background, things that are too close to the camera look very bright. You can make the mid-tones smaller by moving the Midtones tool up. If the graph has a central peak and only a few pixels on the left and right, drag the Midtones slider lower to make the midtones bigger.

8. Click the OK button. You can use the Output Max and Output Min controls on the left side of the histogram to make artsy effects. There is a black circle for the Min slider and a white circle for the Max slider inside the gray square. You can make the image's lightest pixels darker by moving the Max tool down. To lighten the darkest pixels of the image, move the Min slider up. The Max and Min numbers, which range from 0 to 255, change the horizontal axis even though the sliders are moving up and down. All pixels that are outside the range are changed so that they are inside. From the Edit drop-list, you can choose a different color component to make changes.

Spread light over a photograph

- Go to **Adjust** > **Brightness and Contrast** > **Equalize Histogram**.

Expanding the histogram, contrast can be increased

- Click on **Adjust**, then **Brightness and Contrast**, and finally **Histogram Stretch**.

The Histogram Stretch command moves the lightest pixel up to white and the darkest pixel down to black. This command doesn't change images that already go from black and white to black and white. The original image pixels that are very close to being black and white will not change much when you use this command. When you use this command on original images that are very flat (not even close to being black and white), you will see a difference.

Make adjustments to the contrast, brightness, and gamma all at once

1. Click on **Adjust**, then **Brightness and Contrast**, and finally **Levels**.
2. **Choose the color channel you want to change in the Levels group box from the Channel drop-list:**
   - **RGB** lets you change the red, green, and blue channels of a composite histogram.
   - **Red**—you can only change the red channel.
   - **Green**—you can only change the green channel.
   - **Blue:** This button only lets you change the blue channel.
3. **Change the white, black, or diamond-shaped sliders, or use the controls below them to enter numbers.**
   - Move the black diamond slider to the right to make the darkest parts of the image darker, or use the numeric control to set a value.
   - Move the gray square in the middle to the left or right to adapt the image's mid-tones, or enter a number to set a value.
   - Slide the white diamond slider to the left to make the image's darkest pixels lighter, or use the number control to set a value.

Note: Keep pressing Ctrl while moving the black or white diamond slider. This will show you which pixels are being cut off. In the After pane, you can see the colors that were cut.

4. Click the OK button.

You can further do the following:

- **Automatically adjust the photo's contrast:** just click the Contrast button in the Auto group box. **Note**: Click this button if you like the colors of the picture but want to make the contrast stronger.
- **Automatically change the photo's white balance:** Just click on the color button in the box for the auto-group.
- **Automatically change the color and the contrast:** To make the color and contrast change on their own, click the Levels button in the Auto group box. **Note**: If you press this button, the photo's black and white points will be found immediately.
- **Set your own black, gray, or white point and then insert the dropper in one of those colors:** Check the **Colors group box** to use that dropper color. Then, move the mouse to a spot in the Before pane (or the picture window) that you are sure is black, gray, or white.
- **Choose the proper black, gray, or white point automatically:** Hold down Alt as you move the mouse to the Before pane or the image window. When the mouse moves over dark, medium, or bright areas, the right color dropper appears.

- **Set percentage values for the Lower Limit, Upper Limit, and Strength settings in the Auto Color Options dialog box:** It's important to note that higher values for the Lower Limit and Upper Limit controls make the automatic settings more stable, while lower values make the automatic settings less risky. Lowering the Strength setting makes the clipping less noticeable.
- **Reset all modified values to the original values:** Click on the "Reset" button that's next to the color droppers. There is a "Reset to Default" button next to the "Save Preset" button that you can click.

When you use the curves, contrast, and levels button in the auto group box of the curves dialog box, you can change the changes you make in the auto color choices dialog box. You can also use the levels command to move the histogram for a picture that wasn't exposed properly. This command can be used before the curves command.

Converting photo pixels to white and black

1. Select **Adjust Brightness and Contrast > Threshold** as the first step.
2. Type or set a number for pixel brightness in the Threshold control (those below the threshold) to show which pixels should be turned white (those above the threshold) and which should be turned black (those below the threshold). The range is from 1 to 255. A Blacker pixel is seen when the numbers are higher, and more white pixels appear when the value is smaller.
3. Click the OK button. Use the zoom setting in the dialog box to change how the picture looks in the Before and After panes.

CHAPTER 8
ADJUST HUE AND THE SATURATION

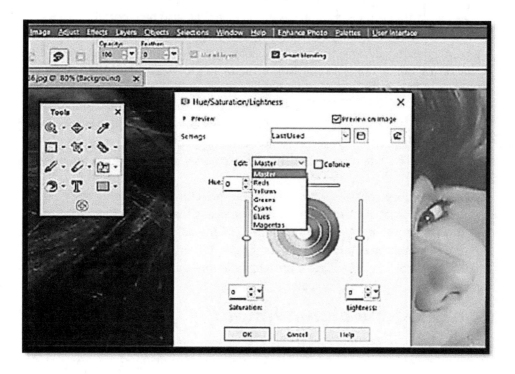

The lack of white in a color shows how saturated it is, which another word for how pure is or bright it is. A color that is 100% saturated doesn't have any white in it. When the saturation number of a color is 0, it is said to have a grayish tint. The thing that makes one color different from another is called the hue. "**Hue**" refers to the color itself, like "**red" or "yellow**." The amount of saturation that a color has tells you how bright it is. Take the hue brilliant orange, which has a high level of saturation. The orange color changes to a rusty hue when the hue and brightness are kept the same. It then changes to a taupe color and finally to a neutral gray color in the middle when the saturation is turned off. The color is taken away when the saturation level is decreased, leaving only the grayscale part. They are pretty neutral and don't add much color, so taupe and mauve are thought to have a low amount of saturation. Fruit apple Colors that have a high-intensity level are red apple and banana yellow. You can think of a color's saturation as how much it stands out from a monochrome version of the same brightness. Improving the saturation in digital pictures can make the colors look more vivid and give the image more "punch," but using too much saturation can distort colors and cause problems like skin tones that don't look natural. Without changing the rest of the picture, you can use the Vibrancy setting to focus on parts of the image that have low saturation. You can also boost the brightness of parts of a picture that already have some color but not a lot of it, so you can change the skin tone without making the whole picture look very different.

You have four options available to you in Paint Shop Pro for modifying the hue and saturation of a selection or a whole image:

- All the colors can be changed to a single color, and the intensity can be changed while the brightness stays the same. Sepia tones, which are the brownish tones found in older images, and other effects that only use one color can also be created.
- You can change any of the colors, as well as their intensity and brightness. Each pixel on a picture goes to a different spot on the color wheel when you change the hue. The blue pixels turn green when the red pixels are changed to green, and the yellow pixels turn cyan when the red pixels are changed to green. If you change the intensity of a color, you can change how much gray it has. It is true that as the saturation number drops, more gray is visible. When you change the lightness, the colors' hue and intensity change.
- You can also change more than one color. One thing you could do is change all the greens to blues. If you change these numbers, all the colors will change, even the ones that were there before.
- With the Vibrancy control, you can change the picture so that only the colors with the least amount of saturation are changed. The pixels that already have a lot of saturation will stay the same. In the end, the intensity of the colors in a picture will be better, but not so much that the colors will look too bright. When adding saturation to a picture, the Vibrancy control is best because it protects skin tones and makes it less likely that you will oversaturate and ruin the skin color of the subject.

Create a duo-tone picture/photo

1. You can find Colorize in the Adjust menu, which is next to Hue and Saturation. Before you choose the Colorize command, you need to do the following: Go to **Image** > **Grayscale**, and then choose **Image** > **Increase Color Depth** > **RGB - 8 bits/channel** from the drop-down menu that shows. This will make a duotone with more subtle color shifts.
2. **This is where you can type in numbers or set parameters:**
   - **Hue:** This property sets the color to which all other colors are changed.
   - **Saturation:** This option sets how saturated the color chosen is.
3. Press the OK button.

Make adjustments to the lighting, color, and saturation

1. To make your choice, go to Adjust, then Hue and Saturation, and finally Hue/Saturation/Lightness. It shows a conversation box called Hue/Saturation/Lightness. The outermost color ring in the dialog box shows the values of the colors in the image as it was first saved. The changed numbers will be shown on the color ring in the middle.
2. To move forward, pick one of these choices from the Edit drop-down menu:
   - Choose Master to change all the colors at once.
   - Use the drop-down menu to change a certain color range. Choose reds, yellows, greens, cyans, blues, or magenta

The control ring that shows up between the inner and outer color rings can be used to change the range of colors that will be changed if you choose the option to Edit Color Range. The range width can be changed by moving the two outside points on the control ring. You can change the area where the change has the most effect by dragging the two middle bars. The change will have the most effect between the bars.

Simply drag the white circles around to relocate the adjustment area.

3. Adjust the Hue slider. The Hue value tells you how much the pixel's color has changed from where it started. This is done by counting how many full turns the color wheel has made. A positive number shows that the rotation is going clockwise, while a negative number shows that the rotation is going counterclockwise. To give you an example, when the Hue number is 180, blue turns into yellow, and green turns into magenta.
4. Set the amount you want by dragging the Saturation slider. As the saturation goes up, move the slider up. As it goes down, move the slider down. You can choose from -100 to 100. When the value is 0, the default settings stay the same.
5. Adjust the slider located under Lightness. The lightness can be changed by moving the slider up or down. Moving the slider down will make it darker. You can choose from -100 to 100. When the value is 0, the default settings stay the same.
6. Click the "OK" button. You can turn a picture into a duotone, also called a two-color image, by checking the Colorize box. This turns the picture to grayscale. You can also add color to the picture by picking a hue and then changing how bright and saturated it is.

Change the hues

1. In the **Adjust Hue and Saturation** menu, choose **"Hue Map**." Keep in mind that the 10 original colors are shown in the row of color boxes at the top of the Hue Shift group box, while the changed colors are shown in the row of color boxes at the bottom. There are 360 degrees on the color wheel, and each color is shown by a different number of turns around the wheel.
2. Make changes to the sliders for each color whose value you want to change.
3. Click the "OK" button.

You can further:
*   **Adjust the saturation levels of every color:** In the Saturation shift control, you can type in a number between –100 and 100, or you can use a figure that's already there.
*   **Adjust the levels of darkness in all colors:** Change how dark all the colors are by typing a number between -100 and 100 into the Lightness shift control or changing the value manually.
*   **Reset the colors to their default settings:** To get the colors back to how they were originally set, choose "Default" from the "Load Preset" drop-down menu.

Remove and adjust the noise

People who take pictures use the word "**noise**" to describe pixels or groups of pixels that are in the picture but don't belong there. The noise could be caused by some things. Most of the time, the problems are caused by either the camera's electrical parts or the file types, like JPEG. Various color flecks can be seen in the image and they stand as noise. You will be able to see the noise better if you zoom in. For example, a picture of a clear blue sky might have spots of color in the red, pink, green, and yellow ranges. Paint Shop Pro lets you get rid of different kinds of noise in a lot of different ways. You can even add noise to an image that is otherwise "**clean**."

You can make the following adjustments to a picture by applying them to either a selection or the whole image:

- You can make a picture look blurry and lose some of its detail at the same time. It's possible to make a picture look better by hiding small flaws and scratches that you can't get rid of with other tools. To make the image look more realistic, just add some noise.
- Using this method, you can find and get rid of small scratches that are lighter or darker than the rest of the surface.
- There is a common problem with video capture photos that can be fixed. It shows up as even and odd-numbered scan lines being recorded at different speeds. The issue may be noticed if the subject was moving when the image was taken. Keep in mind that getting rid of scan lines might make noise stand out more.
- The original look of a JPEG image can be brought back. When you use any software (like scanning software) to save a file to the JPEG format, the information inside the file is compressed to make the file smaller. Any of these effects can be caused by the compression: halos or color leaking past the edges of objects; checkerboard patterns on smooth backgrounds; or blocky areas. Patterns that you don't want can be taken out of scanned pictures. This problem can happen with digital photos that were copied on rough paper. You can fix it by getting rid of single-pixel spots that are mostly black or white.
- If the brightness of each pixel is measured and then compared to the brightness of the pixels around it, noise can be removed from a picture without losing information on the edges of the picture.
- You can get rid of random little dots or noise areas that stand out from the rest of the image. This changes the brightness of each pixel so that it matches the median brightness of the pixels around it. If there are different intensities, the median intensity is the number in the middle. It is not the average. If you want to keep the edges of the object, you can use the Median Filter command. If the pixel you're working on is very different from the pixels around it, you can make more changes to it with this command than to pixels that are similar to nearby pixels. You can tell the program how many pixels will be used in the calculation from the pixels next to it. More information will be lost if you choose a high number of pixels because more noise will be chopped out.
- This method can get rid of multiple black or white spots, like those made by dust on film or video.

- You can clean up a picture by getting rid of dust and noise while keeping the background features that make the picture unique. For example, you could eliminate the noise from a part of the image (like the person's face) while keeping the textures on their clothes. The instructions for One Step Noise Removal and Digital Noise Removal are also available for you to use.

Add noise

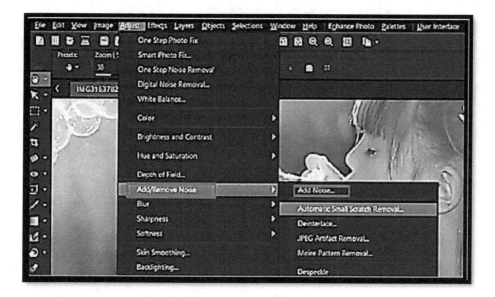

1. Select "**Add/Remove Noise**" from the "**Adjust**" menu.
2. **Pick a noise pattern from the ones that are given:**
   - **Random** gives a granular effect that gives the whole look more depth.
   - The color of the noise is changed by **uniform** so that it looks like the pixels that were there before.
   - When you choose **Gaussian** instead of Uniform, most of the noise will look more like the original images.
3. You can either type a number into the Noise control or pick one from the drop-down menu to set the amount of noise to add.
4. Click the "OK" button. Checking the Monochrome box will let you use black-and-white noise pixels. To use colored pixels, take the tick out of the box.

Auto remove scratches

1. **Add/Remove Noise > Automatic Small Scratch Removal** is what you need to do from the **Adjust** menu.

2. **Mark one or both of the following boxes with a checkmark:**
   - The "**Remove Dark Scratches**" feature can get rid of scratches that are darker than the background.
   - The "**Remove Light Scratches**" option can get rid of scratches that are lighter than the background.
3. The Local Contrast Limits group boxes let you change the amount of contrast between a scratch and its background. You can either type in values or choose values for the Lower and Upper controls. Raise the Lower control until it's just below the point where scratches start to show up again. Cut the Upper control's value down until it's just above the point where you can see the scratches again.
4. **Choose a choice from the "Strength" drop-down menu to change how well the scratch removal works:**
   - Mild
   - Normal
   - Aggressive

Note: Keep in mind that you should choose the lowest setting that can get rid of scratches. Make sure you look at the whole picture to make sure you don't miss any important information.

5. Click the "**OK**" button. You can limit the change to a certain area by making a decision. The command works significantly better when applied to a selection than when applied to the whole image.

Improve the quality of the pictures captured on video

1. **Add/Remove Noise** > **Deinterlace** is what you need to do from the **Adjust** menu.
2. Use the drag handle in the top pane of the dialog box to move to the part of the image where the scan lines are easiest to see. This could be the Before or After pane.
3. In the box that says "Scanlines to keep," pick a choice that tells you whether to keep the scan lines with odd or even numbers.
4. Click the "OK" button.

You need to use the Deinterlace command on the image before you can try to resize it. It's harder to tell the difference between individual scan lines when an image is resized because more or fewer pixels are added or taken away. If you've already shrunk your image, you need to get it as close as possible to its original size, making sure that the height of each scan line is exactly one pixel. To change the size of the image so that each scan line is one pixel high, use the zoom control in the dialog box to get a better look at how many pixels are in a scan line. Then, you can change the size of the image to suit your needs. To give you an example, you would cut the image in half if the bigger version had scan lines that were two pixels high. Keep in mind that when you change the image's size, it becomes less clear.

Remove Artifacts from every JPEG picture

- Select **Adjust > Add/Remove Noise > AI Artifact Removal**.
- Click "OK."

This will depend on your machine and the size and complexity of the picture. The AI (artificial intelligence) study and use of the results may take a few seconds or so. You can see how far along the AI analysis is by looking at the green progress bar at the bottom of the program window. You can use the AI Artifact Removal tool on any kind of file, and it will work. Even if you change the format of a JPEG picture to Paint Shop Pro (.pspimage), you can still use the command. Some information about JPEG images is lost when they are compressed, which makes it hard to restore them.

Eliminating patterns of moire weave

1. From the "**Adjust**" menu, choose "**Add/Remove Noise**," and then choose "**Moire Pattern Removal.**"
2. By entering or setting a number in the Zoom control, you can make the image bigger so that you can see the fine details.
3. You can either type a number into the Fine details control or choose one from the drop-down menu to set the level of pattern removal. One small change at a time should be made to the number until the pattern can't be seen anymore. If you raise the value, the image might become less clear, so pick the lowest value that still gets rid of the pattern.
4. You can make the picture less big by using the zoom setting in the dialog box. Keep doing this until you can see color bands or blotches in the After pane. Please keep in mind that

bands or blotches might be visible when the picture is at 100%, but they might stand out more when the level is lowered.

5. You can change the value of the Remove bands control one at a time until any color blotches or bands are less noticeable. They might not go away completely. Use the lowest value possible to keep very small objects from losing their color.

6. Click the "OK" button.

After you get rid of the moire pattern, you might be able to use the Sharpness commands in the Adjust menu to bring back detail and get rid of blurriness. This will not stop the pattern from being used again, though. When you use the Moire Pattern Removal dialog box, the Sharpness commands will work best if you set the Fine details slider to a value that is a bit higher than what is needed to get rid of the pattern.

Remove lone-pixel specks

1. Pick out the area of the picture that has the specks.
2. Click "**Adjust**," then "**Add/Remove Noise**," and finally "**Despeckle.**"

Eliminating noise while maintaining the boundaries of the image

1. Find the place where the noise you want to get rid of and click on it.
2. Open the "**Adjust**" menu, click "**Add/Remove Noise**," and then click "**Edge Preserving Smooth.**"
3. To change the "Amount of smoothing" value, type a value or change the one that is there already. The image should still have all of its original detail, so choose the least amount of smoothing that will do the job. You can't enter a number that is either greater than or equal to 1.
4. Click the "OK" button. If you want to use the Edge Preserving Smooth command on the whole image, you can, but it works better when you only select the problematic area.

Removing certain portions of the noise

1. Find the place where the noise you want to get rid of and click on it.
2. Select "**Add/Remove Noise**" from the "**Adjust**" menu then select "**Median Filter.**"
3. You can manually set or enter a value in the Filter Aperture control to choose how many pixels around the middle pixel intensity should be used in the calculation. With even numbers between each value, the range goes from 3 to 31. **Note**: Use the least processing power that can still get rid of the noise if you want to keep the image's details. To make specks of single pixels of color, set the filter to 3.
4. Click the "OK" button. You can use the Median Filter command on the whole picture, but it will work best if you only pick out the area that is giving you trouble.

Removing multi-pixel specks

1. Find the area where the specks are and click on it.
2. From the "**Adjust**" menu, choose "**Add/Remove Noise**" > "**Salt and Pepper Filter**.

3. Use the Speck size control to enter a value or choose one from the drop-down menu to set the minimum size in pixels of the largest speck that can be removed. This value never has an even number.
4. You can enter or set a value in the Sensitivity to specks control to set how different an area must be from the pixels around it to be considered a speck.
5. Click the "OK" button.

You can apply the Pepper Filter command to the whole image if you want to, but it is better to first choose the area that needs fixing. Checking the box that says "**Include all lower speck sizes**" will get rid of all the specks that are smaller than the Speck size value. By checking the box that says "**Take aggressive action,**" you can make the correction more severe.

Eliminating noise while maintaining the original textures

1. Search for the area with the noise you want to get rid of and click on it.
2. Go to the "**Adjust**" menu, pick "**Add/Remove Noise**," and then pick "**Texture Preserving Smooth.**"
3. Type a number into the Amount of correction control or choose a number from the drop-down menu to change the amount of correction. A very small amount of the noise is gone when the number is lowered, but the textured parts are still there. When the value is raised, more noise is removed, but it's possible that some textured areas won't be kept fully.
4. Click the "OK" button.

Manage the depth of the field

AI Portrait Mode adds a background with a realistic depth of field and artificial intelligence (AI) to identify people in your images. It is possible to change the depth of field effect by changing the blur, bokeh, focus range, and feather.

To use AI Portrait Mode's depth of field effect on portraits

1. Open an image that is in portrait mode.
2. Go to **Adjust** > **Artificial Intelligence** and choose **AI Portrait Mode**. After a short time, the AI will look at the picture and open the AI Portrait Mode window.
3. Look closely at the parts of the background that have a red accent. Take note that there is a safety zone around the subject. When blur is added to the background, this buffer helps the subject keep its sharp edges.
4. If you need to make the selection even better, choose one of these choices in the Brush Mode section:
   - **Add to Subject**—takes away the red overlay on the subject.
   - **Remove from Subject:** This feature adds a red overlay over parts of the image that you want to be background. You can change the buffer area all over by dragging the Expand Border tool. **Note**: Hold down Alt and move the Brush Size tool to change the

size of the brush in the preview window.

5. When you're sure you want to go with your choice, click **Next**.
6. To change what happens by default, you can change any of the following controls:
   - You can choose between circular and hexagonal aperture shapes under the blur and aperture form choices to get nice bokeh effects in photos with light spots.
   - The focus range feature lets you finetune the size of the in-focus area,
   - and the feather edge feature changes how soft the edge is along the subject.
7. Click "Done." If you right-click and drag, you can switch between the Add to Subject and Remove from Subject brush modes.

Select an area of focus

To quickly choose a focus area in PaintShop Pro, you can make a selection that is either round or square, or you can trace a selection around an area to get a unique shape. You can also flip a choice.

Adjust blurred area

You can change the blur that is applied to the area outside of the pick, as well as the way that the blurred area moves into the focused area. Furthermore, Paint Shop Pro lets you pick either a round or a hexagonal aperture shape. The form of the aperture may affect the light patterns that show up in the areas that aren't in focus. This effect, which you can best see as tiny bright spots against a dark background, is called bokeh.

Create a focus area with the Field of Depth effect

1. From the Edit tab, pick the area you want to keep in focus.
2. Click on **Adjust** and then **Depth of Field**.
3. Use the Blur tool to change how much blur is added to the area that isn't in focus.

You can further:

- **Invert the chosen area:** Check the Invert box.
- To change how the area that is in focus and the area that is blurred change. Pick a button from these:
  - Circular Aperture Shape
  - Hexagonal Aperture Shape
- **Adjust the movement between the area in focus and the blurred area**: Move the slider to change the feather edge. When you move the scale to the right, the feathering gets stronger. When you move it to the left, it gets weaker. You should know that a setting of 0 makes the edge rough and hard to define, which is probably not what you want. In general, don't move this scale below 2 or 3.
- **Adjust the size of the area in focus**: The Focus range slider can be moved to the left to make the focus area smaller. Moving the slider to the right will make the edge of the pick

stand out.

If you don't already have a selection, you can use the Circular, Freehand, Rectangular, or Raster Selection tools in the Depth of Field dialog box to pick a focus area. Before you use the Focus range scale to change the selection's edge, make it a little bigger than the area you want to keep in focus.

Blur images

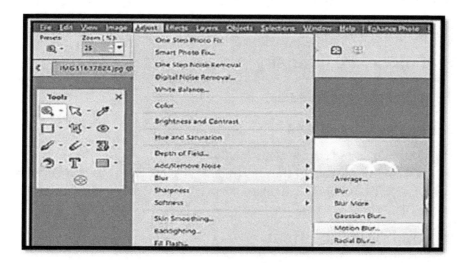

Various commands in Paint Shop Pro help you blur your photographs. The following adjustments may be made to a layer, a selection, or the full image:

- You can get rid of noise in a picture by making each pixel as bright as the pixels around it on average. You can also be able to get rid of the color blurring that happens when a palette picture is changed to 24-bit color depth.
- To get rid of the noise, you can lower the contrast and make the changes in your picture smooth.
- You can change how strong the blurring effect is by gradually blending a certain number of pixels while following a bell-shaped curve. The haze has a thick middle and a thin edge.
- Use a set exposure time to make it look like you're taking a picture of something moving.
- To make it look like you're taking a picture, you can make the camera spin in loops or zoom in very quickly while the shutter speed is very slow.

What is the purpose of blurring an image?

You can soften a pick or picture, fix a shot, or get rid of noise in an image by use of blurring commands. The Blur command lowers contrast and smooths out transitions by combining the pixels close to the edges and in areas with big color changes. If you use any of the Blur orders more than once on the same picture, the effect will be stronger.

Apply a blur that is determined by the intensity of neighboring pixels

1. Choose Adjust, Blur, and Average.
2. Enter or set a number in the Filter aperture control. The numbers range from 3 to 31 in odd-numbered steps. As the number goes up, the blur gets worse.
3. Click the OK button.

Use just a trace amount of blurring

- Go to **Adjust > Blur and Blur**.

Use blur of moderate intensity

- Go to **Adjust > Blur and Blur More**.

Use a Gaussian blur effect

1. Go to **Adjust > Blur** and choose **Gaussian Blur.**
2. The Radius control lets you set the area (radius) around which pixels are dimmed. You can either type a radius or enter a number. It can be anywhere from 0.00 to 100.00.
3. Click the OK button.

Utilize a radial blurring effect

1. Go to **Adjust > Blur** and choose **Radial Blur**.
2. In the Blur Type group box, pick one of the options below:
   - **Spin:** This blurs pixels in a circle around the picture's center.
   - The zoom and twirl effects blur pixels. Zoom moves pixels out of the middle of the picture. You can change the level of the twirl by typing or adding a number into the Twirl degrees control.
3. In the Blur group box, type a number into the Strength control. The effect is stronger when the number is higher and weaker when it is lower. If the radius needs to be shrunk to fit the picture, check the Elliptical box. This option blurs pictures in a circle when they are rectangular; it does not affect square images.
4. To move the image's center, type a number into the Center group box for the following controls: You can choose how much to blur the image's center with Protect center%; Horizontal offset% lets you set the blur's horizontal center point; Vertical offset% lets you set the blur's vertical center point. As the value goes up, the radius of the unblurred center area gets bigger.
5. Click the OK button.

Sharpen images

The majority of digital images need to be sharpened because digital cameras make pictures soft during the capture process. Shots that need to be sharpened can also be caused by moving the camera during the capture. Digital cameras are more likely than film cameras to make images that are slightly out of focus. This problem is usually easy to fix. Most of the time, changes to color, tone, and size make images less clear, so it's best to sharpen them before printing, sharing, or storing them.

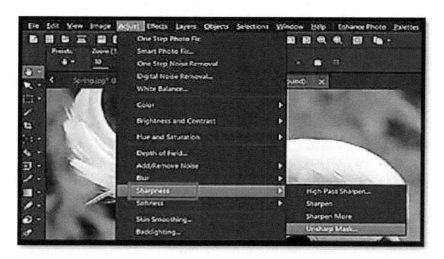

PaintShop Pro's sharpening tools make blurry photos look better by increasing the contrast between pixels that are close together.

You can sharpen a selection, a layer, or the whole image with the following commands:

- You don't have to focus on low-frequency things like big structures, patterns, and background colors. Instead, you can focus on high-frequency things like edges.
- You can make an image clearer and sharper by increasing the contrast between pixels that are close to each other, especially around the edges of the picture.
- It is possible to sharpen the image's mid- to high-contrast lines without making the noise worse, which is not what most professional color correction, does.

Increase the amount of sharpness you use

1. Go to **Adjust** > **Sharpness** > **High Pass Sharpen**.
2. To set the area (radius) around which pixels will be sharpened, you can put a number between 0.00 and 250.00 into the Radius control. **Note:** Images with soft details and close-up objects usually require higher Radius settings; images with lots of fine detail, on the other hand, usually require lower Radius settings.
3. In the Strength control, type a number between 0 and 100 to choose how strong the order

is overall.

4. **Pick one of these options from the Blend mode drop-down menu to decide how the brightened high-frequency areas will be blended into the main picture:**
   - More contrast is made by Hard Light than by Overlay. This takes away the image's neutral tones and makes edge features stand out.
   - **Soft Light:** This setting makes photos look softer.
5. Click the OK button.

How to do a modest amount of sharpening

To sharpen, go to **Adjust** > **Sharpen** > **Sharpen**. If you choose the command again, the effect will be twice as strong.

Utilize both low and high-frequency sharpening techniques

1. Go to **Adjust Sharpness** and choose **Unsharp Mask**.
2. In the Radius control, type a radius (distance) between 0.01 and 100.00 to set the area (radius) around which pixels are sharpened. **Note**: Images with soft details and close-up objects usually require higher Radius settings; images with lots of fine detail, on the other hand, usually require lower Radius settings.
3. In the Strength control, type a number between 1 and 500 to find the overall strength of the command.
4. In the Clipping control, type a number between 0 and 100 to find the lowest lightness level needed to sharpen pixels close to each other.
5. Click the OK button.

Softening images

A good soft-focus lens can make an effect that can be copied by relaxing a photo and making it look dreamy and shiny. Photos that are clear and sharp look softer when you add a soft focus.

The following techniques for softening are offered by PaintShop Pro:

- You can add a soft-focus camera lens effect to the image or selection, or
- You can blur the image or selection in a soft, even way.

Give a picture or a selection of a soft-focus effect

1. Go to **Adjust** and choose **Softness** > **Soft Focus**.
2. **In the Focus group box, enter a number in the following fields:**
   - The adjustment's strength is based on the adjustment's softness. The image isn't changed much at smaller percentages. As the percentages go up, the image gets blurry.
   - **Edge importance:** This factor tells the program how much to soften the edges of the image. At smaller percentages, the edges are not as sharp. The edges get less

flattening because they are kept at higher percentages.
3. Type a number or a letter into the control that goes with it in the Halo group box.
   - The degree of halo effect is based on the amount. Lower numbers only add the halo to the brightest parts of the image. Higher numbers make all the bright areas look like they have a halo around them.
   - **Halo size:** This decides how big the halo is. At lower levels, the circle isn't very big. At higher settings, you can see the halo effect.
   - **Halo visibility:** The halo vision factor tells you how strong the halo visibility is. At lower settings, you can hardly see the halo effect. As the numbers go up, the halo effect stands out more.
4. Click the OK button. If you check the box next to Include dispersed light, you can soften parts of the background that are too bright.

Resize pictures

After you've made changes, you can change the size of your picture. It is very important to know how scale affects picture pixels.

The result of changing an image's resolution to a lower value

Pixels can be any size in terms of their shape. One pixel for each color makes up a single-color sample. Resampling an image means changing the number of pixels in it. This can happen when the picture is resized. During resampling, the file size changes. Print density (ppi) is the number of pixels that fit on an inch. Better print resolution means that the pixels and pictures that are written are smaller. A smaller print size makes the pixels bigger and the picture has a bigger resolution. By resizing (not resampling), you can change the print quality and size while keeping the file size and number of pixels.

- Change the file size and number of pixels while keeping the print quality and size the same (resampling).
- Change the file size, print quality, size, and number of pixels

When you change the size of your photos, remember these tips:
- When you expand a picture, you might lose some of its clarity and detail. Choose options that are powered by AI (artificial intelligence technology) for the best results.
- Change the size of a picture only once. If you changed the picture's size by accident, undo it and try again.
- Photos should be fixed and improved before size changes.

Re-sampling techniques

With the Resample option, you can decide how the pixels in an image are changed. It takes the most time to use the Bicubic method, but it usually gives the best results.

Here are the resampling types you can use in PaintShop Pro:

- **AI-Powered:** When you enlarge a picture (the new size is bigger than the original), this type of resampling keeps the details. It uses artificial intelligence (AI).
- **Smart Size:** Pick the best formula based on the bigger or smaller pixels you choose.
- **Bicubic:** This plugin reduces the jaggedness that can happen when pictures are too big, moving around, or difficult.
- **Bilinear:** The two pixels closest to each current pixel are used by Bilinear to decide how new pixels will look.
- **Pixel Resize:** Adding or removing pixels to get the picture's width and height you want (best for simple graphics and images with sharp edges).
- **Averaged Weight:** Figures out how new pixels will look by looking at the average color values of pixels that are close to them (useful for making images less photorealistic, skewed, or complicated).

What happens to pixels on image resampling?

When you use the Resize command to make the image bigger, data from the current pixels must be interpolated into new pixels. Let's say you have a picture that is 100 × 100 pixels and you want to make it bigger by adding 200 x 200 pixels to the picture. You begin with 10,000 pixels and end up with 40,000 pixels when you scale. This means that the last three-quarters of the images are "made up." One popular way to fill in missing pixels is to interpolate the gaps between pixels that are left over when the picture's dimensions are increased. The Pixel Resize method copies the color of the closest pixel. The bilinear method uses an average of four pixels that are close together (from a range of 2 2 pixels). The more complicated Bicubic method uses 16 pixels next to each other, starting from an area of 4 4 pixels. The colors in the fake pixels might look better because the larger neighborhood shows more precisely how the color changes in that part of the picture. When you use the Resize command to make the image smaller, the colors of the pixels are averaged. Think about making a picture 50 x 50 pixels instead of 100 x 100 pixels. Each of the 2,500 pixels in the result shows a quarter of the pixels that made up the original picture. Different resampling methods change how much weight is given to the original pixels when they are combined.

Is there another method for resizing images that I may use?

You can change a picture's size in more ways than just the Resize command. You can change the frame size, crop it, print it at a different size, use the Copy Special command, or save it for Office. As the frame size grows, more pixels are added to the edges of the picture. When the canvas size is shrunk, pixels close to the edges of the picture are covered, but all of the layer information is kept. When you crop a picture, the pixels that are not in the crop area you choose are taken away. You can change the size of a picture you send to the Print Layout window by dragging its selection handles. Print the picture in different sizes, this way of changing keeps the image file the same and doesn't change it. The Copy Special command allows you to copy the image to the Clipboard in one of three sizes, depending on whether you are printing the picture professionally, printing from your desktop, copying to your computer screen, or copying to an email. Once you've copied the image to the Clipboard, you can paste it into a file in a different program, like a word processor. You can set the picture's size and resolution and save the file to disk with the Save for Office command. Other than that, it has similar resizing choices to the Copy Special command.

Resizing images

1. Go to **Image** > **Resize**.

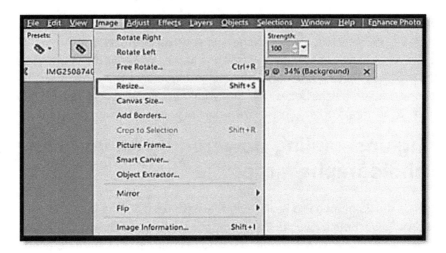

2. **Choose one of the options below to change the size:**
   - You can set the size in pixels with the "**By Pixels**" choice. Just type numbers into the "Width" and "Height" boxes. You can also pick from a list of popular sizes in a drop-down menu.
   - As long as you put a percentage in the Width or Height box, you can change the size by that percentage (compared to the original).
   - By Print Size: In this option, you can put values in the Width and Height boxes to set a size in millimeters, centimeters, or inches. You can also change the Resolution number and pick a standard size from a drop-down menu.
   - If you choose "Depending on One Side," the picture will be resized based on how it looks now. You can pick the width or height in pixels.
3. Check the box next to Advanced and AI-Powered Settings, and then make any of the following changes to make it even more unique.

You can further:

- **Resample image pixels:** The image's pixel measurements are changed by resampling, which lets you change the resolution setting without changing the width or height settings.
- **Sharpen the picture after scaling:** Tap the "Use Resamples" box, and then go ahead to

pick "Bicubic" from the list. Set the Sharpness setting to a number between 50 and 100 to make a picture bigger or smaller. When the Sharpness control is set to 0, the picture that is expanded stays as sharp as before.

- **Maintain the image's brightness after resizing it:** Mark the box that says "Preserve picture brightness when resizing" in the "Miscellaneous" section of the "General Program Preferences" window.
- **Unlock the aspect ratio:** Take a checkmark out of the Lock aspect ratio box.
- **Resize just the chosen layer:** Just uncheck the box that says "resize all layers."

The Width, Height, and Resolution controls interact with one another when the Resample using the checkbox is not selected. If you change one control, it affects all of them. When you use this method, the size of the image's pixels stays the same. When you change the aspect ratio, you distort the image by making one dimension bigger or smaller than the other. There is a lock icon next to the width and height boxes that lets you know if the aspect ratio is locked. If you check the box next to Maintain original print size, you can keep the image's current print size.

Utilizing upsampling powered by AI, you can make your photographs larger

When you use the PaintShop Pro Resize window to make a picture bigger (called "upsample"), AI-powered choices become available. Other options that use artificial intelligence (AI) look at your image's pixels and add new ones so that the result is sharper and more detailed than with regular upsampling. Normally, you might not be able to use low-resolution photos, but this can help. You might have an old JPEG picture from a bad camera, or you might have a photo that has been cut to show something important, but the resolution is too low to print. Keep in mind that GPU acceleration can sometimes make AI research go faster. Different choices may give you different results, so try a few to find the best one for your computer. For AI-powered upsampling, the largest pixel size that can be used is 10,000 x 10,000 pixels. If the dimensions are bigger, you can't use this option because the settings are turned off.

Increasing the size of the picture with the use of upsampling powered by AI

1. Go to **Image** > **Resize**.
2. **To enlarge the image, choose one of the choices below:**
   - You can set the size in pixels with the **"By Pixels"** choice. Just type numbers into the "Width" and "Height" boxes. You can also pick from a list of popular sizes in a drop-down menu.
   - As long as you put a percentage in the Width or Height box, you can change the size by that percentage (compared to the original).
   - By Print Size: In this option, you can put values in the Width and Height boxes to set a size in millimeters, centimeters, or inches. You can also change the Resolution number and pick a standard size from a drop-down menu.

- If you choose "Depending on One Side," the picture will be resized based on how it looks now. You can pick the width or height in pixels.
3. Check the box next to Advanced Settings and AI-Powered Settings.
4. Tick the box next to "Resample utilizing" and pick "AI-Powered" from the drop-down menu.
5. **In the Mode area, choose one of the options below:**
   - **Photorealistic:** Choose this choice when you take a picture.
   - **Illustration:** Select this choice if you want to use other illustrations or drawings.
6. You can pick how much noise reduction to use. Moving the slider to the left will keep the finer features of the pixels. Moving it to the right will make the edges smoother.
7. Based on what your computer needs, choose whether to turn on or off GPU Acceleration.
8. Click the OK button. There is a green progress bar at the bottom of the program window that you can use to see how the AI research is going.

Working with materials and colors

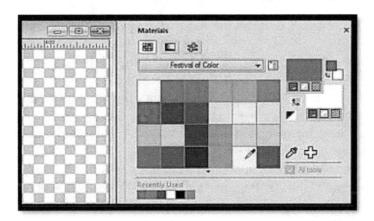

It's important to know how to pick colors and handle materials in PaintShop Pro whether you're coloring a picture, making a website, or making scrapbook pages.

Using Materials Palette on your PaintShop Ultimate

You can paint, draw, and fill using a variety of styles and materials with PaintShop Pro.

- Material is made up of style and an optional texture.
- A style is a color, gradient, or pattern.

You can choose between styles and materials in the Materials menu. You can always get to the Materials bin. It can stay open while you work, or you can only show it when you need to. You can also switch the colors or elements of the foreground and background.

Central components of the Materials palette

- The Swatches tab displays color swatches for the currently chosen scheme. You can save and use swatches again and again.
- Click on the HSL Map tab to see the Saturation and Lightness box. In this box, you can change the color that is currently selected or pick a new color by moving the Color (hue) bar.
- **Slider's tab:** The sliders and value boxes on the sliders tab let you pick a color in the RGB, HSL, CMYK, Lab, and Web safe color spaces. You can also use grayscale to make a shade.

Both the foreground and background materials are shown in the Foreground and Stroke and Background and Fill Properties boxes. The style (color, gradient, or pattern) and possible texture make up the materials. Clicking any box will open the Material Properties dialog box, which is where you can change the settings for the material.

The following applications are possible for these boxes:

- Background items can be used for fills and foreground items can be used for brush strokes.
- When you use a brush to make strokes, including the fill tool, clicking lets you paint in the center and right-clicking lets you paint in the background.
- When you use the Art Media tools, you can pick the background color for the pigment you put on the paper.
- When you use vector text or forms, you can pick a background color for the fill and a foreground color for the outline.
- The foreground and background color boxes show you the current foreground and background colors while letting you choose colors that don't affect the text.
- **Style button:** This shows the style that is being used right now, which could be a color shift, a pattern, or both. The most recent color, tint, and pattern can be changed by clicking the Style button and picking a different style from the drop-down menu. These settings are turned off for the Art Media tools, which only use flat colors.
- The foreground turns black and the background turns white when you press the Set to Black and White button. The background button turns on or off the current background. This is helpful when using the Edit Selection tool.
- The translucent button lets you choose whether the information in the background or foreground is see-through. Text and vector images are often put on clear materials. In a transparent foreground, only the objects or letters are filled in. In a clear background, there is no fill; only the objects or letters are dashed. This button can't be used by tools that need a foreground or background.
- The "All tools" checkbox shows if the features in the foreground and background are used for all tools. If the box is not checked, the checked materials only apply to the present tool.

Why are both color and properties boxes found on the Materials palette?

You might be wondering why there are color boxes in the Materials palette when you can click on the Foreground and Background Properties boxes to choose colors. You can use the color boxes to quickly change colors without changing anything else. That is, you can pick a different color even if the characteristics box shows a design or gradient. Instead of the color in the color boxes on the Materials menu, the brush paints with the gradient, texture, or pattern that is shown in the characteristic boxes. Choose Color from the Style choices in the Foreground and Background Properties boxes. This makes the colors in the color boxes work.

Show or hide the Materials palette

- Choose **View** > **Palettes** > **Materials**.

If you want to close the panel even more, you can press F2 or click the Close button in the title bar.

Change or alter the colors or materials of the foreground and the background

To switch between colors or materials in the materials menu, press the "Swap" button.

Select colors from the dialog box for material properties

In Paint Shop Pro, changing images often involves picking a color before painting, drawing, or filling an image, making changes to colors manually, or picking a background for a new raster picture. If you're making your color scheme, the Color page in the Material Properties dialog box gives you the most options for choosing colors. Color patterns can help you choose colors that look good together. The Color page comes up when you click on one of the Foreground/Stroke Properties, the Background/Fill Properties, or one of the two smaller color boxes. If you click the Color box in a different text box, the same thing takes place. This page's look is based on the picture's color depth (16 bits/channel, 8 bits/channel, 256 colors, 16 colors, or 2 colors). For example, when working with palette colors, you can't use the Wheel, Slider, or Color Harmonie choices. Instead, you see samples of the colors.

There are several options to choose colors on the Color page:

- **Wheel**: When you click the Wheel button, the Color (hue) wheel and the Lightness meter show up.
- **Slider**: If you click on the "Slider" button, a drop-down menu with sliders and value boxes for the color space will appear. You can pick from Web Safe, Lab, RGB, HSL, CMYK, and Grayscale.

- **Swatch:** If you press the swatch button, a color swatch palette will appear. If you don't want to see the Standard Palette, you can choose any other unique palette from the drop-down menu.
- **Color Harmonies:** You can choose from five color harmony settings that make it easy to find a group of colors that go well together. These are Complementary, Triad, Tetrad, Analogic, and Accented. Mono is the best choice for a single color.
- On the bottom left of the Color page, you can see the color swatches that go with them. Choose a color swatch and click "Add to Palette" to add it to your custom palette.
- HTML color code lets you type in HTML color values. There is a Color tab in the Materials Properties box. What to do:

1. **Choose one of the following actions in the Materials palette:**
   - To pick a foreground color, click the Foreground and Stroke Properties box or the Foreground Color box.
   - To pick a background color, click the Background and Fill Properties box or the Background Color box. Click the Color button to go to the Color page.

2. **Pick one of these:**
   - Click on the color wheel and then on a color to get a close match. To change the intensity, move the color indicator from the middle of the circle to the edges. To make the color darker or lighter, move the tab on the Lightness bar to the left or right. This bar is to the right of the color wheel.
   - Click Slider to choose a color space from the drop-down menu. You can move the buttons or type numbers into the boxes to choose the color you want.
   - Click Palette to bring up a drop-down menu and choose a palette. Then, click a color swatch to choose it.
   - In the HTML text field, type in a hex color number.

3. Click the OK button. You can also pick a lot of colors by using color harmonies.

You can also: You can select color harmony buttons that are complementary, triadic, tetradic, similar, or accented. On the bottom left of the Color page, you can see the color swatches that go with them. Move the color dot around the color wheel to change the colors. Click on a color swatch and then click "Add to Palette" to add it to your own color palette. Besides that, there is a color choice in the Materials palette where you can pick one. Check the box next to "All-tools" on the Materials window to make all tools use the same colors. If you uncheck this box, the present materials will only be used by the active tool.

Choose Colors for Palette Pictures

Palette images are pictures that have a color range of 2 to 256. You can't use the Color page to pick the foreground and background colors for palette shots. Instead, you need to use the Materials palette.

Using palettes to choose colors for photographs

1. **The Materials palette lets you do one of the following:**
   - To change the color of the foreground, click the Foreground and Stroke Color box.
   - To change the color of the background, click the Background and Fill Color box. The Color page and palette are opened when you click on a color box.
2. **To arrange the colors, pick one of these options from the Sort order drop-down menu:**
   - **Hue:** Sorts by color
   - **Palette:** sorts by the order of colors in the palette
   - **Luminance:** sorts by brightness
3. Pick a color.
4. Click the OK button.

To make sure that the Materials palette only shows the colors that can be used for palette photos, the Show document palette setting must be turned on. In File > Preferences > General Program Preferences, find the list of palettes and choose Show Document Palette from the drop-down menu.

Choose Colors from the desktop or an image

You can pick a foreground or background color from any open picture or color in Paint Shop Pro. This could be a color on a menu. This choice is useful if you want to match the colors of the Windows screen or use the color of a certain icon. You can also pick a color from other browser-based apps or websites. You can use the Sample and Fill mode to take a sample of color from a picture and then use that color as a fill in a different area or image.

Using the Dropper tool, you choose colors from the currently active image

1. Pick up the Dropper tool from the Tools bar.
2. **Make the following changes to the Tool Options panel:**
   - **Sample Size drop-list**: The Sample Size drop-list lets you pick how many pixels to sample.
   - **Use all layers**: If you check this box, a sample will be taken from all of the picture layers.
3. Click on a color in a picture with the left mouse button to make it the foreground or background.

If you hold down Ctrl and click on the picture, you can choose a color for the foreground or the background. You can also choose a color from the image when you use the Paintbrush or the Eraser tool.

Fill and Sample with colors selected with the Dropper tool

1. Pick up the Dropper tool from the Tools bar.
2. Press the Sample and Fill button in the Tool Options window.
3. In the picture box, click the color you want to try. The tool icon changes right away into a full icon.
4. Click on the spot where you want the sampled color to go and pick it. The last settings for the Flood Fill tool determine how the fill spreads and reacts with the background.

Choose your colors from the desktop

1. Make sure the screen shows the color you want.
2. In the Materials box, click the **Sample Color button**.
3. Move your mouse to the part of the screen that you want to change the color of. This group includes other open windows or Web pages that can be seen.
4. Pick out the area you need to fill with the sampled area. When the mouse is moved over areas that can be sampled, the Sample Color dropper icon shows up.

CHAPTER 9
USING THE PATTERNS

Painting, drawing, or filling patterns with color can give them interesting results. People who use PaintShop Pro can pick from many themes, such as ones with bricks, stained glass, and zebra stripes. Another way to make patterns is to use a picture or a part of an image. The pictures you've made look more unique when you use patterns. You can make text with patterns, items with patterns on the edges or fills, and brush strokes with patterns. Patterns let you make tiled images that can be used on websites, as well as greeting cards and other paper goods. For projects like CD covers, diaries, and greeting cards that need pretty backgrounds, patterns are very helpful. You can find patterns online for free.

How are patterns and textures distinct from one another?

Using the Materials palette, you can pick whether to add a pattern or a texture to a material. What exactly makes them different from each other? A pattern is a picture that is not clear, repeats itself, and has certain colors and shapes. Shapes and colors that don't change are also styles, just like patterns. The foreground and background colors that are being used right now are not being used by patterns. For example, if you choose the Bricks patterns and then use the PaintBrush tool to make brush strokes, each stroke will paint the whole brick pattern. A texture gives fabric or paper the look of having a textured surface. As of right now, the textures are in style, like a solid color. If the background color is yellow and you choose the Crumpled Paper texture, each brush stroke will paint yellow with the crumpled paper texture on top of it. You can use a texture along with when a single color, gradient, or pattern is being used. This means that you can choose a pattern and a texture at the same time if you want to.

Applying present pattern

- To use the pattern that's already there, go to the Materials menu and click on the Pattern button. It will be in the Style drop-list for either the Foreground and Stroke Properties box or the Background and Fill Properties box. The pattern that was chosen most recently will be used from now on.

Choose patterns

1. **Any of the following should be chosen in the Materials panel:**
   - When you click on the Foreground and Stroke Properties box, you can pick a foreground pattern from the list.
   - There are different background patterns you can choose from when you click the Background and Fill Properties box.
2. Pick out the pattern you want to use.

3. Click the small picture of the pattern you want to use on the Design page.
4. Make any changes you need to the following controls:
   - **Angle:** This number, which can be anywhere from 0 to 359 degrees, shows the pattern's angle, or direction.
   - **Scale:** The scale of the image's real size can be set. The range is from 10 to 250. It's more likely that the picture will show up more than once in the pattern when the number is lowered. There is a chance that the picture will be cropped or lose detail and become fuzzy when the number is raised.
5. Click the "**OK**" button.

You can further do the following:

- **Save the pattern as a swatch that you can view in the future:** Click the Add to Palette button.
- **Use the most recent resources for all of the tools**: Mark the "All tools" box on the Materials panel with a check mark. If you uncheck the box next to it, the materials will only be used on the active tool.

The angle of the pattern can also be changed by moving the control needle over the pattern image on the Pattern page. You can find this on the Pattern page.

Work with a selection or an active image as a pattern

1. Open the picture you want to use.
2. First, decide which part of the picture you want to use as the pattern by making a pick. Design thumbnails can be seen on the Pattern Page of the Material Properties dialog box. These are small versions of the design.

Save your images as patterns

1. Use PaintShop Pro or a similar tool to make a picture.
2. Save the picture file in the Patterns folder of the PaintShop Pro application folder or **Documents/Corel PaintShop Pro/2023/Patterns**. The pattern can be seen in the drop-down menu called Design on the Pattern tab of the Material Properties dialog box.

If you want to change the directory where pattern files are saved by default, click the More Options button and then choose File Location from the menu that comes up.

Use Textures

It's possible to make cloth or paper look like it has different textures by painting, drawing, or filling with a texture. To make strokes and fills for the foreground and background, you can mix textures with the current color, gradient, or pattern. When you use PaintShop Pro, you can choose from a lot of different textures, such as clouds, cracked sidewalks, and old paper. You can also start with a picture and make your own patterns.

Applying current texture

To use the chosen texture, click the Texture button in the Foreground and Stroke Properties box or the Background and Fill Properties box on the Materials panel. It will start using the most recent image you chose.

Pick a texture

1. **Choose one of the following actions to carry out on the Materials palette:**
   - Choose a foreground pattern from the list when you click the Foreground and Stroke Properties box.
   - Click on the Background and Fill Properties box and pick a background texture from the list. Now, a box called Material Properties will show up.
2. Select the texture you want to use.
3. Click the "Add Texture" box on the page where you want to see the texture.
4. Click on a texture icon to choose it.
5. Make the necessary changes to the following settings to change the texture:
   - **Angle:** If you set this value to a number between 0 and 359 degrees, it tells you the angle (or direction) of the texture.
   - **Scale:** The scale of the image's real size can be set with scale. The range is from 10 to 250. It's more likely that the picture will show up more than once across the texture when the number is down. There is a chance that the picture will be cropped or lose detail and become fuzzy when the number is raised.

The style and look of the content that will be made will be shown in the Current preview box while you make changes to these parameters.

6. Click the "OK" button.

You can further do the following:
- **Make adjustments to the presentation of the content:** After hitting the Color, Gradient, or Pattern buttons, changes the settings.
- **Use the most recent resources for all of the tools:** Mark the "All tools" box on the Materials panel with a check mark. If you uncheck the box next to it, the materials will only be used on the active tool.

You can use many strokes or fills to make the pattern darker and fill it in. To do this, use the lines or fills more than once. The angle of the texture can also be changed by moving the control needle in the Pattern page image of the texture. This is one of the choices you can make.

Saving photos as textures

1. Use PaintShop Pro or a similar tool to make a picture.
2. You can save the picture as a BMP file in either the Textures folder in the PaintShop Pro application folder or the Documents/Corel PaintShop Pro/2023 folder. You can see a

sample of the texture on the Texture page of the Material Properties dialog box. It's called Texture. There are previews for all of the files in the Textures folder of the PaintShop Pro application folder.

Note: Press the "More Options" button and pick "File Location" from the menu that comes up. You can change where the texture files are saved by default using the drop-down menu.

Working with Swatches and Custom Color Palettes

A swatch will be added to a palette that is only for you when you save it. You can make more than one color. Like, you could use a custom palette to keep track of all the colors and supplies you need for a certain job. It is possible to get rid of panels that you don't need anymore. After making one in PaintShop Pro, you can now load your color scheme. For example, a company might work together on how to use its brand colors by using a palette with custom swatches. In the same way, cartoon artists can share palettes, and graphic designers can use one of the pre-loaded palettes to get ideas.

Swatches

You can save a style or material as a swatch so that you can use it again later. A swatch is made by mixing colors, gradients, patterns, or textures. When you are working on a project, swatches help you remember the color choices, design styles, and types of materials you like best so that you can find them more quickly. You can choose swatches and make changes to, delete, or rename them. You can also change how the swatches are shown, which another choice is. The area where the palette is kept also holds the group of swatch files (.pspscript). You can save palettes as groups. Otherwise, if you don't change anything, you can find them here: It's possible to find swatches in the [C]: Users [name of user] Corel PaintShop Pro 2023 Documents...

Choose color palettes

1. In the Materials panel, find the Swatches tab and click on its button.

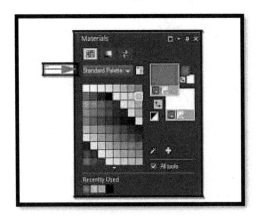

When you click the Palette selection menu, a drop-down menu will appear. Choose a color scheme from that menu.

Create palettes

1. In the Materials panel, find the **Swatches tab** and click on its button.
2. Click the "More Options" button and then choose "New Palette."
3. Give your palette a name, and then click OK to move on.

There is a drop-down menu above the images that has the palette in it. You can now add swatches to the menu. By default, the color scheme is always saved in the [C:] folder.

Importing a palette of swatches

Take action in one of the following ways:

- For the default user, move the folder that has the palette and the.pspscript files for each swatch in the palette to the following location: This file, Swatches, can be found at [C: Users [user name]DocumentsCorel PaintShop Pro2023].
- Copy the palette folder, which has the .pspscript files for each swatch in the palette, to a different location. Then, go to the location where you saved the palette folder by going to **File** > **Preferences** > **File Locations**, clicking on Swatches in the list of file types, and clicking **Add**.

Create swatches

1. Click on the button next to the Swatches tab in the Materials box.
2. Pick out the color you want and click the "Add to Palette" button.
3. In the "Add to Palette" box, pick out a palette to add to your collection. Then, click "OK." You can also click the "New" button to make a new palette.
4. You can name your swatch by typing it in the box that says "New Swatch." You can see the name of a swatch in the Materials menu when you move the cursor over it and read the tooltip that comes up.
5. Press the "OK" button.

Note: On the Materials panel, you can alternatively click the **More Options button** and then choose New Swatch from the drop-down menu that appears.

To choose a swatch

1. In the Materials panel, find the Swatches tab and click on its button.
2. One of the things below must be done:
   - Right-clicking on a swatch lets you choose it as the background.
   - Clicking on the swatch you want to use as the foreground material makes your choice.

Editing a swatch

1. In the Materials panel, find the Swatches tab and click on its button.
2. Double-click the color you want to change in a swatch to make changes.
3. Change the style (color, gradient, or pattern) and texture of the material to make it look different.
4. Click the "OK" button.

You can also click on the swatch, then on the More Options button, and finally pick Edit Swatch from the menu that comes up.

Delete swatches from palettes

1. In the Materials panel, find the Swatches tab and click on its button.
2. Click on the swatch you want to get rid of to select it.
3. Press and hold the "Remove from Palette" button.

Rename swatches

1. In the Materials panel, find the Swatches tab and click on its button.
2. Click on the swatch whose name you want to change.
3. Click the "More Options" button, and then choose "Rename Swatch" from the screen that comes up.

When you get to the Materials palette, select the Swatches tab and carry out the options from the below:

- **Choose which swatch types are shown:** When you click the More Options button, a drop-down menu will show. Choose View from that menu to see a certain type of swatch.
- **Modify the order in which the swatches are sorted:** Click the More Options button and a menu will appear. Choose Sort By from that menu to sort things by style or name. By default, this is how the colors will always be set up.
- **Modify the sizes of the swatch thumbnails:** When you click the "More Options" button, a drop-down menu will appear. Choose Small Thumbnails, Medium Thumbnails, or Large Thumbnails from the list that comes up. Thumbnails of a middle size will be shown by default.

CHAPTER 10
LAYERS IN PAINTSHOP PRO

When you work with layers in PaintShop Pro, you can make creative effects and illustrations, add things to your pictures, and edit them more easily. You can also add elements to your pictures. There are several ways to mix the pixels of the layers, add new ones, remove old ones, and change the order in which they are stacked. Each layer can be changed separately, and the changes won't affect the others unless you combine them. Corel PaintShop Pro caters to both photographers and digital artists, integrating layers into its editing workflow to offer unparalleled versatility and creative control. Each layer type serves a distinct purpose, **facilitating the application of various effects and adjustments tailored to specific editing needs and artistic expressions.**

- The **background layer** serves as the foundational element of an image, typically containing raster data and positioned at the bottom of the layer stack. While imported JPEG, GIF, or PNG images automatically generate a background layer named "Background" on the Layers palette, images with transparent backgrounds create a raster layer as their bottom layer, allowing flexibility in layer organization.
- **Raster layers** represent the most fundamental layer type, storing information using pixels. These layers are commonly utilized for artwork, photographs, and pixel-based editing tasks, offering precise control over individual pixels. Conversely, vector layers store instructions for drawing lines and curves, enabling the creation of scalable shapes, text, and other vector-based elements. Unlike raster layers, objects within vector layers can be manipulated independently without affecting other elements on the layer.

105

- **Adjustment layers** provide a non-destructive method for modifying the color and tone of underlying layers, allowing experimentation with various color corrections and combinations without altering the original image layers. Popular adjustment options include levels, curves, brightness/contrast, and hue/saturation/lightness, offering extensive control over image enhancements.
- **Mask layers** are invaluable tools for selective editing, allowing users to reveal or conceal portions of underlying layers by adjusting layer opacity. This feature enables precise adjustments and enhancements to specific areas of an image, directing focus and emphasizing key elements within the composition.
- **Art media layers** simulate traditional artistic mediums, offering unique properties akin to a canvas surface. Automatically created when using art media tools such as the smear or oil brush, these layers facilitate artistic expression and experimentation.

The Layers palette

This serves as the central hub for managing layers, providing a comprehensive set of commands and options for layer adjustment and organization. Familiarizing oneself with this palette is essential for harnessing the full potential of Corel PaintShop Pro, enabling seamless layer manipulation and creative exploration.

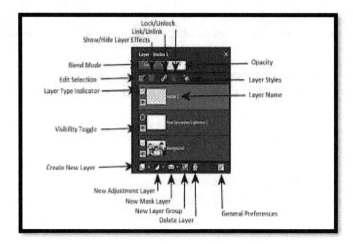

- **Blend Mode –** Change the blend mode to adjust the way that the selected layer blends with the layers underneath it. Great for compositing and special effects.
- **Edit Selection –** This button will highlight the selection you've made on your image and enable you to adjust your on screen selection using various tools or brushes.
- **Layer Type Indicator –** Displays the type of layer you're working with, including Background, Raster, Vector, Adjustment, and Mask, as well as whether the layer is the parent layer of a group.
- **Visibility Toggle –** If the eye is showing that layer is visible. Click on the eye and the layer will still be there but invisible until you click on the eye again.

- **Thumbnail –** A small picture of the layer's contents. You can click the thumbnail to drag and drop layers to change their order within the image or even drag them to another open image. Objects or text on layers closer to the bottom will appear "underneath" those layers closer to the top of the list if they overlap in the image.
- **Create a New Layer –** Click this icon to create a new layer. A pop-up menu will appear with layer options so you can select the layer type you want.
- **New Adjustment Layer –** Enables the ability to change the color or tone of the underlying layers. All layers are affected underneath an adjustment layer (unless clipped). This is our suggested method when it comes to applying image adjustments in PaintShop Pro because adjustment layers are non-destructive and can be changed at any time.
- **New Mask Layer –** Use this button to add a layer mask to the currently selected layer. This will enable the ability to paint away parts of your layer without damaging your original image.
- **New Layer Group –** An option that helps keep related layers together for organizational purposes or editing purposes. For example, you could group a text layer and speech bubble graphic layer so that they can be moved and resized as a single unit. Grouped layers are put into a folder. You can choose multiple layers and put them in a group, or create a new group by clicking this icon. Layers can be dragged in or out of groups.
- **Delete Layer –** Select the layer you wish to delete and then click this icon to remove it and all of its contents from the image.
- **General Preferences –** This will open a pop-up menu that provides some program options. The same menu can be accessed through File > Preferences > General Program Preferences.
- **Layer Name –** This is the customizable name you can give to each layer. Single left-click to select the layer, then single left-click again to rename the layer. You can also double-click the name to open the Layer Properties menu where you can change various options associated with the layer.
- **Layer Styles –** With this feature, you can create visually interesting and creative effects for a layer in real-time, and you can fine-tune the effect before applying it. The Layer Styles feature provides six effects: Reflection, Outer Glow, Bevel, Emboss, Inner Glow, and Drop Shadow.
- **Opacity –** Determines the transparency of a layer. A setting of 1 makes the paint or layer to be nearly transparent. A setting of 100 makes it completely opaque.
- **Lock/Unlock –** The padlock means the layer's transparency is locked. Transparent areas remain protected when you paint, apply effects, paste selections, or make other modifications. The transparency lock feature applies to raster layers only.
- **Link/Unlink:** Enables the ability to link layers to have them move together on the image canvas when you move one layer with the Move tool. You can link grouped layers and individual layers from different groups so they all move in relation until they are unlinked.
- **Show/Hide Layer Effects –** Use this button to hide all layer effects and show only the background layer, click again to show all layers again.

Layers in Action

Now that you've grasped the concept of layers, their types, and how to manipulate them through the Layers palette, it's time to explore how layers can elevate your work. Layers offer endless creative possibilities, allowing you to experiment with various techniques and combine elements in innovative ways. Consider this just the beginning of your journey into the realm of layers. As you become more proficient, you'll uncover new techniques and discover exciting ways to leverage the power of layers in your projects. So, let's dive in and explore the boundless potential that layers bring to your creative endeavors.

Exposure Blending

Exposure blending is a powerful technique commonly employed by landscape photographers to balance the exposure in their images. By combining multiple photos taken at different exposures, photographers can capture details in both the highlights and shadows, resulting in a more balanced and visually appealing image. To execute exposure blending, you'll need two photos taken from the same position but at different exposures—one properly exposed for the sky and another for the foreground. With the help of layers in photo editing software, such as PaintShop Pro, you can easily blend these images. Start by layering the properly exposed sky photo over the foreground photo. Then, create a mask layer, allowing you to selectively reveal parts of each layer by painting with a brush. With the properly exposed foreground as the base layer, use the brush to paint out the sky, unveiling the detailed clouds and vibrant colors from the sky photo. This process seamlessly merges the two images, resulting in a final image that showcases the best of both exposures. Unlike automated exposure merging techniques, exposure blending gives you full control over the blending process. By manually painting on the mask layer, you can precisely control where and how the blending occurs, ensuring a natural and visually stunning result tailored to your creative vision.

Local Adjustments

Local adjustments are a powerful technique in photo editing, allowing you to fine-tune specific areas of an image while leaving the rest unchanged. With layers, you can selectively apply adjustments such as saturation, brightness/contrast, and sharpening, providing precise control over the final result. To make local adjustments, start by creating a new layer with the desired adjustments applied. This layer serves as the base layer for your edits. Then, using a brush tool on a mask layer, selectively reveal the adjustments only in the areas you choose. This method grants you flexibility in targeting specific elements or regions of your photo for enhancement. This layer-based approach is versatile and can be applied to various editing tasks. For instance, you can adjust individual elements like white balance or completely replace backgrounds. In the provided example, multiple layers are used—one for the foreground (hills and grass), another for the sky, and two adjustment layers for altering contrast and brightness. By meticulously blending and revealing layers, you can achieve seamless and impactful edits tailored to your creative vision.

Make your photos fun!

Using layers in your photo editing endeavors opens up a world of creative possibilities. Whether you're crafting scrapbook pages, embellishing photos with frames, or adding decorative elements using picture tubes, layers provide the flexibility and control to achieve your desired results. For instance, picture tubes allow you to easily decorate your photos stroke by stroke on separate layers, while layer manipulation enables seamless object removal and insertion into new backgrounds, as demonstrated with the winter-themed photo featuring your niece. These examples only scratch the surface of what you can accomplish with layers. As a best practice, it's wise to duplicate the background layer before diving into edits, ensuring you always have a pristine copy to revert to if needed. This precautionary step provides peace of mind and allows for experimentation without the fear of irreversibly altering your original image.

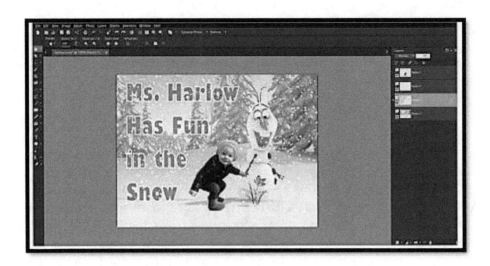

Promote the Background Layer

The Background layer can be turned into a standard raster layer so that it works the same way as the other layers in your document. Raster layers can be moved to any other spot in the stacking order, and they can also be made transparent. Select the Background Layer from the Layers menu and click on the Promote Background Layer button to make it a normal raster layer. You can also right-click on the layer and pick "**Promote Background Layer**" from the menu that comes up.

Delete Layers and Clear Layer Contents

You can either delete everything on a layer or take it out of the picture completely. Even if you delete what's on a layer, the layer itself stays in the picture. The background color and material are filled into the background layer, and the raster and vector layers become see-through.

Erase layers

1. Pick out the layer or group of layers you want to get rid of in the Layers panel. You can also pick the layer group.
2. Click the "Delete Layer" button to get rid of a layer. You can also:
   - Use the Delete option in the Layers menu to get rid of the layer you've picked: Choose **Layers > Delete**.
   - **Delete a chosen layer by right-clicking:** To delete a layer, just right-click on its menu and choose "Delete."
   - **Delete a chosen layer by dragging:** Just drag the layer to the button that says "Delete Layer."

Clear a layer's contents

1. Go to the Layers panel and click on the name of the layer you want to remove. Make sure that nothing is chosen on the layer that isn't being shown.
2. Go to the menu and choose Edit > Clear.

Note: You can also press the Delete key on your computer to get rid of a layer.

Duplicate and Copy Layers

It is possible to copy a layer that is inside a picture. As long as the original layer stays intact, you can try out different changes and effects on the copied layer. You can also use the duplicated layer as a base for a new layer that you make. If you drag a layer into another picture, it will be copied there. You can also copy and paste it. There is no difference between these two ways.

Duplicate layers inside your image

First, pick out the layer you want to copy. Then, go to the Layers menu and pick out "Duplicate." The layer that was copied is added right on top of the layer that was picked. You can right-click on the name of the layer and pick "Duplicate" from the menu that comes up. You can also copy the layer by going to **Edit** > **Copy** and then **Edit** > **Paste as New Layer** to make a new layer from the copied layer.

Make copies of layers to use in another picture

1. Pick out the layer you want to duplicate in the Layers panel and click the **Copy button**.
2. Move the mouse to select "**Edit**" and then "**Copy**."
3. Click the "**Open**" button to open the picture where you want to add the layer. If there are layers in the picture, use the mouse to pick one. Once you put the cloned layer, it will show up on top of the currently chosen layer.
4. Go to the menu and choose Edit > Paste as New Layer. The layer is put in the middle of the board and pasted there.

Make copies of the layers, and then paste them into another picture

1. Go to the Edit tab and open both files.
2. In the Layers menu, drag the layer you want to copy from one picture to the tab of the other picture. After that, when the second picture is active, drag the copied layer to where you want it to be in the Layers palette.

The Edit tab needs to be in the mode that shows tabbed documents (Windows > Tabbed Documents) so that you can drag and drop layers over pictures.

Rename Layers

It might help to give each layer a new name as you add it to a picture. This way, it will be easy to find them in the Layers box. It will be easy to work with the picture after this.

1. Click the layer you want to change the name of in the Layers box. Then wait a moment and click it again.
2. Type the new name into the box and press the Enter key.

If you want to change the name of a layer, you can double-click on it to open the Layer Properties dialog box and type a new name in the Name field. You can also right-click on the layer and pick "Rename."

View Layers

You can change which layers, layer groups, and vector items inside the picture you can see. People who look at the picture can still see the layers that can't be seen. You can also change which layers are shown and which are hidden.

Conceal or show a layer

- Click the Visibility Toggle button for the layer you want to show or hide to put it on or off. This button is next to the name of the layer.
- The Visibility Toggle button when the layer can be seen.
- The Visibility Toggle button when the layer can't be seen. There are layers inside a layer group that are hidden when you hide the group itself.

To see only the active layer, go to Layers > View > Current in the drop-down menu.

Conceal or reveal all of the layers

Check the following:

- **See all layers:** Pick **Layers**, **View**, and **All**.
- **Hide all layers:** Pick **Layers**, **View**, and **None**.

Invert hidden and visible layers

- Choose **Layers > View > Invert**.

Everything that was seen before is now hidden, and everything that was hidden before can now be seen.

Find Layers

For projects that are very complicated and have a lot of layers and layer groups, you can use the Quick Search tool to quickly find a layer by its name.

Search for layers using the names of their layers

1. Find the Show/Hide Quick Search button on the Layers palette and click it. This will open the Quick Search box at the very top of the palette.
2. Type a word or phrase into the box. Every layer is hidden except for any layers or sublayers that have the search term in them in some way.
3. If you want to see all the layers without the search results seen, click the X icon in the "Quick Search" box.

Organize Layers Using Color

You can organize the layers palette visually by choosing different colors for the layers and groups of layers in the palette. You can see that the color that is being underlined is the background color of the icon to the left of the layer or group name. This does not affect the picture itself. Any child layers in a layer group that doesn't have their highlight colors set are given the color of the parent layer. You can use the same highlight color for all the layers in a group, or you can use a different color for each level in a separate group.

Make adjustments to the highlight colors for the layer icons

1. Double-click the layer in the Layers palette to bring up the Layer Properties box. The menu will show up.
2. Click on the box next to Highlight in the Layers Palette title.
3. Choose the color you want from the list that shows up next to the check box.
4. Pick a color and click "OK."
5. In the Layer Properties dialog box, click the OK button. The color that is highlighted is shown next to the icon.

Note: If you right-click on the color box and choose a color from the drop-down menu that appears, you can choose a color to highlight colors that you have used lately.

Change the Sequence of Layers in a picture

How a picture looks depends a lot on the order in which its many layers are drawn. One easy way to rearrange the layers in a picture is to use the Layers menu to change the order in which the layers are packed. If a layer or layer group has parts, like vector objects or grouped layers, all of those parts move with the layer or layer group when the stacking order changes.

Changing the order of layers or layer groups

Choose the layer or group of layers on the Layers menu and drag it to a different spot in the stack. Changing the order of groups or layers of layers. There will be a green line showing where the layer is as you move it. When you move one of the layers around, the pointer turns into a hand. If the cursor shows a null symbol, it means that the item that was chosen cannot be moved to the place that is currently chosen. You can also move a layer or group of layers by going to the Layers menu, choosing "Arrange," and then choosing the action you want to take.

Move Layers on the Canvas

If you stay inside the picture canvas, you can move the items of a whole layer to anywhere you want. If you move part of a canvas layer, the layer will not be cropped. Instead, you can either move the part back onto the canvas or make the canvas bigger to show the area that was hidden in the first place.

Make adjustments to the canvas layers

1. Pick out the layer you want to move in the Layers panel and click the **Move button**.
2. Choose the **"Move tool"** from the "Tools" menu.
3. Drag the layer inside the picture to where you want it to be. You can move layers around with the Pick tool as well as pick them.

Group Layers

Layer groups can be made so that many layers can be put together. Using layer groups, you can organize the Layers palette and change the properties of each layer, like opacity and blend mode, for the whole group. You can also limit the effects of adjustment and mask layers to the layers below the active layer instead of the whole image. Finally, you can delete all layers in the group, move all grouped layers together in the stacking order, and so on. There must be at least one layer in each layer group. These layers can be raster, vector, art media, mask, or adjustment layers. Masks can also be in layer groups. When one layer group has another layer group inside it, you have a nested group. PaintShop Pro can delete a layer group if all of its layers are changed or deleted.

Make use of the layer groups

1. To start, open the Layers menu and pick the first layer you want to add to the group. This layer will be the base one.
2. In the Layers panel, find the drop-down menu and choose **"New Layer Group"** from it. The layer group is made, and the chosen layer is added as a member of the layer group.

There will always be a number after the word "Group" in the name of the layer group, like "Group 1."

You can also:

- **Using the Layers palette, add a layer inside of a layer group:** Drag a layer from the Layers menu into a group to add it. (A thin black line shows you where the layer is while you drag it.)
- You can add a layer to a layer group from the Layers menu: **Layers** > **Arrange** > **Move into the group** is what you need to do.
- **Set a layer group so that it is contained within another layer group:** Moving a layer group from the Layers menu to another layer group by dragging it will do the job. (A thin black line shows you where the layer group is right now as you move it.)
- Drag a layer down to the bottom of a layer group to put it there. To begin, drag the layer down to the second-to-last spot on the screen. Drag the layer at the bottom up one level. Remember that if you drag a layer straight to the bottom of a layer group, it will go outside of the group instead of inside it.
- **Using the Layers menu to create a layer group:** Choose **Layers** > **New Layer Group**. In the Layer Properties dialog box, change the scales and checkboxes as needed. Finally, click the OK button to finish.

Take out layers from the groupings

Just move the layer somewhere else that isn't in the layer group. You can get rid of the layer from a group even more by going to **Layers** > **Arrange** > **Move out of the group**.

Separate the individual layers

To get rid of a layer group from the stack, select it and then go to the Layers menu and choose "Ungroup Layers."

Link Layers

You can link layers together so that they move on the screen at the same time when you use the Move tool to move one layer. You can connect grouped layers so that the individual layers inside a group can move on the picture canvas at the same time. You can also link layers from different layer groups together and then move those linked layers together without moving any of the other layers in the layer group.

Does the sequence of stacking change in any way when linking is used?

There is no change to the stacking order when you link. Instead, linking only affects how you move the picture canvas with the Move tool. In the stacking order, the only way to move layers closer to each other is to group them. All the layers in a group will move if you move that group up or down in the stacking order, even if the layers are not linked to each other.

Link the many layers

Go to the Layers panel and pick out the layers you want to link. Then click the Link/Unlink button.

Unlink the layers

To unlink a layer, select it in the Layers palette and click the Link/Unlink button. The layer no longer has the icon that stands for the link.

Layer groups may either be unlinked or linked

Select the layer group from the layer menu that you want to link or unlink, then click the button that says "Link or Unlink Group." If you select a related group, the button on the toolbar will be highlighted. If you select an unlinked group, the button will not be highlighted. If you double-click on a layer group, the Layer Properties dialog box will appear. In this box, you can check or uncheck the box that says "The Group is linked and then click "OK when you're done.

Blend Layers

You can get some cool effects by changing how the pixels on one layer mix with the pixels on lower levels. In PaintShop Pro, you can select from a large number of blend modes. The picture will automatically show the blended pixels, but the different layers will still be shown as before. When layers are mixed, the default blend mode for each layer is Normal. When this mode is used, pixels are put together based on the layer's brightness. The layer that was picked will be mixed with all the layers below it, not just the layer that is right below it. You can change more than just a layer's blend mode. You can also change that layer's blend range. By default, the blend mode will be used on all pixels. Based on the blend range, the blend mode can only change a certain number of pixels. Blend ranges let you change a layer's opacity based on its brightness or color channel. By doing this, colors are taken away from the layer you chose, making room for other colors.

Set a layer's blend range

1. Double-click the layer in the Layers menu to open the Layer Properties dialog box. The choices will show up.
2. Click on the Blend Ranges tab to open it.
3. Use the **"Blend Channel"** drop-down menu to pick a channel to work with while combining layers. If you want to use the brightness values of layers to figure out how opaque they are, choose the Grey Channel. If you want to base the layer's opacity on a color channel, pick either the Red Channel, the Green Channel, or the Blue Channel.
4. If you drag the arrows above the slider, you can change the options where the opacity is

100%. In this case, you can set a layer's opacity to 100% anywhere between 43 and 126 in terms of brightness. As you move toward the brightest and darkest values, the opacity gradually decreases.

5. To make the options where the opacity is 0%, move the arrows below the slider.
6. Click the "OK" button.

Set Layer Opacity

If you change a layer's opacity from its default value of 100% (which makes it completely opaque) to 0% (which makes it fully transparent), you can get some very interesting effects. When a layer is only partly solid, you can see the layers below it through the crack. One more thing you can do is change the opacity of a layer group. The Opacity choice on the Layers palette can be used to change how transparent each layer is. Different pixels have different levels of opacity, which is different from the visibility of the layer as a whole. For instance, if the opacity of a pixel is initially set to 50 percent and the opacity of the layer is also set to 50 percent, the pixel will seem to be 25 percent opaque. If the layer is part of a layer group that is configured to have an opacity of 50 percent, then the pixel will seem to have an opacity of 12.5 percent.

Altering the opacity of layer groups is another one of your available options

1. Pick out the layer or group of layers you want to work with in the Layers panel.
2. You can change the opacity by dragging the slider to the amount you want.

Note: This is an extra way to change a layer's opacity: double-click the layer, change the Opacity number in the Layer Properties dialog box, and then click OK to save the changes.

Protect Transparent Parts of Raster Layers

With the Lock Transparency feature, you can limit which parts of a raster layer that hold data tools and effects can be used. Clear areas don't lose their protected status when you paint, add effects, paste choices, or make any other kind of change.

Note: The Lock Transparency function can only be used to lock the transparency of raster layers. It is possible to make group layers, vector layers, art media layers, adjusting layers, or mask layers less see-through. Background layers don't have any way to make them see-through.

Lock or unlock portions of raster layers that are transparent

In the Layers panel, pick out the layer you want to lock or unlock, then press the Lock/Unlock button. A Lock/Unlock button will show up on the layer when the transparency is locked. To turn on transparency, just click the button one more time. After unlocking the layer, the icon that was on it will be taken off. If you double-click the layer, check or uncheck the Lock transparency box in the Layer Properties dialog box, and then click OK, you can also lock or open transparent areas.

This will open a new window where you can work with the transparent parts that are locked or otherwise not locked.

Merge Layers

When you flatten a picture, you combine the different layers that make up the image into one. You can choose to merge only certain layers in a picture, or you can merge all of them. When layers are combined, the picture takes up less space in your memory. The process is finished when layers are combined using their blend modes, vector data, and vector text are turned into raster data, and areas of the background layer that were see-through are colored. You can also make a new layer by joining two or more existing ones together. Certain file types, like JPEG, GIF, and TIF, do not allow pictures with more than one layer. If you export a picture in one of these formats, PaintShop Pro will combine all of its layers into a single background layer. The vector layers and art media layers are turned into raster layers when you save a picture in Photoshop PSD format. However, the raster layers of the correction layers and raster layers stay in the image.

Note: As a backup measure, you should always make a duplicate of the original PspImage picture before you join layers. Any changes you make to one layer will not affect the others after they have been combined.

Merge two layers at the same time

1. Move one layer in the Layers panel so that it is right on top of the other layer.
2. Pick the layer that is at the top of the stack.
3. Select Merge and then Merge Down from the Layers menu.

To merge all of the layers, choose **Layers > Merge > Merge All** from the menu bar (Flatten).

Specific layers should be merged

1. In the layers panel, choose the layers you want to merge.
2. Go to the menu and choose **Layers** > **Merge** > **Merge Selected**.

You can also merge layers by right-clicking on any of the layers you want to join and then choosing "**Merge Selected**" from the menu that comes up.

The process of combining certain layers with a new one

1. In the layers panel, pick the layers you want to merge into one new layer.
2. Go to **Layers** > **Merge** > **Merge Selected to New Layer** from the menu that appears.

Right-click on any of the layers you want to merge, go to the Merge menu, and choose "**Merge Selected To New Layer**." This will join the layers you have chosen into a new layer.

Merge every visible layer

1. In the Layers panel, click the Visibility Toggle button next to each layer you don't want to join. This will make the layer visible again. When a layer is hidden, the Visibility Toggle button will look different.
2. Go to the Layers menu and pick Merge from the list. Use the **Merge Visible command** to make a single raster layer out of all the visible layers.

The layers' ability to stay hidden is kept. The information about how transparent the original layers were is kept in the merged layer, which is now the active layer and can be found where it used to be. If the layer you chose is part of a group, the merge action will only change the layers that can be seen in that group. This means that none of the layers in the group will be joined if the layer group is set to invisible. This will make all the layers inside the group invisible.

Merge visible layers with new layers

1. Click the Visibility Toggle button on the Layers palette to hide any layers you don't want to merge. You can then merge only the levels whose names are the same. It will look different when a layer is hidden when the Visibility Toggle button is used.
2. If you want to combine the levels that you can see into one, go to the levels menu and select **Merge**. Select Merge Visible to New Layer from there.

Merging every layer in the group

1. In the Layers panel, pick the layer group or layer that you want to merge.
2. To make a single layer out of all the raster layers in the group, go to the Layers menu and select the Merge option.

Use Adjustment Layers

Correction layers called adjustment layers change the color or tone of layers below them without changing the picture layers themselves. You can also call them correction layers. By adding adjustment layers, you can try out different color changes or different mixes of color changes. You can change, hide, or get rid of adjustment levels. Any changes made to one layer will also be made to the layers below it. When an adjustment layer is part of a layer group, it can only change the layers in the group below it. Set up a layer group with just one layer, and then put the adjustment layer on top of the group's layer. This will let you add an adjustment layer to a single layer without changing any of the layers below it. The layer is the only one in the layer group that is changed.

Include layers of adjustability

1. Click on a layer in the Layers panel to choose it. When the adjustment layer is being used, it will show up on top of the layer that is currently selected.
2. To add an adjustment layer, go to the palette toolbar and select "**New Adjustment Layer."** Next, pick a type of adjustment layer from the list that shows. The sample parts that show up in the first dialog box show the picture before and after you make changes to it. Select

Default from the Load Preset drop-down selection to return the values to their initial, factory-default settings.
3. Go to the top of the window and click on the Adjustment tab to change the settings for the adjustment layer.
4. Click the "OK" button.

Another way to add an adjustment layer is to go to the menu and choose Layers, then New Adjustment Layer. If you double-click on the adjustment layer and then choose the "Reset to Default" button in the Properties dialog box, you can also go back to the original settings.

Adjust the visibility of the adjustment layer overlay

- Go to **Layers** > **View Overlay**.

You can also click the Highlight mask area button on the Layers panel to show or hide the adjustment layer overlay. In the upper right corner of the palette is this choice.

Making changes to the adjustment layers

1. In the Layers box, double-click the name of the layer you want to change. So, this will open the Edit Adjustment Layer box.
2. Click on the "**Adjustment**" tab and change the settings for color or tone fixing.
3. Click on the "**General**" tab to change the layer's name, blend style, and opacity, among other things.
4. Click on the Overlay tab and make changes to the overlay's color and transparency. The layer that looks like a red mask and has a transparency of 50% is the overlay that is used by default.
5. Click the "OK" button.

Note: You can also choose Layers > settings to open the Layer settings dialog box.

Use Layer Styles

You can use a lot of different effects in the Layer Styles tabbed area of the Layer Properties dialog box. These effects can be used separately or together. This tool lets you make creative and eye-catching effects that can be added to a layer in real-time. You can also make small changes to improve the effects. The result before you uses it. You can use the Layer Styles tool to get six different effects: Outer Glow, Drop Shadow, Bevel, Emboss, Bevel, and Inner Glow. If you use these effects on a separate layer and then save the file in a format that allows layers, like the PspImage format, the original picture on that layer stays the same. This is because you saved the file in a type of file that can handle layers. In this sense, adjustment layers and layer styles are theoretically the same. On the other hand, layer styles are only applied to the edges of the levels themselves, not to the canvas below them. This is the main difference between them.

If you change the size of a layer that already has one or more layer styles on it, the effects will change to fit the new size of the layer. The only types of layers that can have layer styles added to them are raster. One type of style for layers is the Drop Shadow style, which is added to the layer's data from the outside. Some layer styles will not be noticeable if the layer in question does not have any clear areas. It is possible to save a layer style as a preset and to copy and paste it between levels in the same project. Layer styles can be saved as a set too. Because of this, it is easy to give different pieces of text or items on different layers the same effect, like a drop shadow, glow, or reflection.

What exactly is the point of having a checkbox labeled "Layer"?

When this box is checked, you can choose to show the layer data along with the effects that have been applied. The layer data can be hidden and only the impacts can be seen when this box is not checked. Taking away the option next to the Layer will make the data for the first layer act like it has a mask on it.

Why does the order include check boxes?

Yes. The effects have to be put together in a certain order for the results to make sense. For example, you wouldn't want to put an Outer Glow effect under a Drop Shadow effect or a Drop Shadow effect on top of the thing that gives it its light. This means that the Reflection effect comes first, then the Outer Glow effect, then the Bevel effect, and so on. One of the last effects that is used is called "Drop Shadow." When we update layers that already have effects applied to them, what kinds of changes may we anticipate? Add new text or shapes to a vector layer to change it, or paint on a raster layer with the brush tool to change it. The effects that were already on the layer are added to any changes you make. Whether you are changing a vector layer or a raster layer, this is always the case.

Apply Reflecting layer styles

1. Select a layer, and then from the menu that shows, select Layer Styles.
2. Click on the Layer Styles tab in the Layer Properties dialog box to open it.
3. In the group box that shows the effects, select the Reflection choice and click the "Check" button next to it. In the After pane, the effects' starting stage has been brought up to date. The "Preview on Image" box must be checked if you want to see how the changes will appear on the real image. Keep in mind that the Reflection effect could create data that goes beyond the picture canvas. If this happens, you may need to make the canvas bigger to see the full effect.
4. The Size slider on the left can be used to change how fast the mirror fades compared to the data from the first layer.
5. To change how light the image is as a whole, move the Opacity slider around as shown.
6. You can move the red Reflection Distance control line in any direction you want to set the horizontal axis around which all layer data is reflected.
7. Click the "OK" button. Setting up a Layer Style is easy. You can save the settings as a preset

and then use that preset to change the settings on any other layer.

Apply Outer Glow layer style

1. Select a layer, and then from the menu that shows, select Layer Styles.
2. Click on the Layer Styles tab in the Layer Properties box to open it.
3. Select the "**Outer Glow**" choice in the group box that displays the effects. There are new changes to the After pane that show the new Outer Glow effect was added. The "Preview on Image" box must be checked if you want to see how the changes will appear on the real image. Keep in mind that the Outer Glow effect could create data that goes beyond the viewable picture canvas. To see the full effect, you may need to make the canvas bigger.
4. Use the Size tool to change how far the glow goes past the layer data. If you click and drag the scale, you can do this.
5. Move the Opacity tool to the left to change how bright the glow is. This will help you see the glow better.
6. Click on a bright color in the rainbow color picker to choose it. The color that is currently chosen is shown in a row at the bottom of the color picker.
7. Click the "OK" button.

Applying the Bevel style to the layers

1. Select a layer, and then from the menu that shows, select Layer Styles.
2. Click on the Layer Styles tab in the Layer Properties box to open it.
3. In the group box that lists the effects you want to use, check the "Bevel" box. The new Bevel effect can be seen in the After pane, which has been updated. The "Preview on Image" box must be checked if you want to see how the changes will appear on the real image.
4. Use the Size tool to set the distance between the edge of the layer data and the edge of the bevel. You can do this by moving the slider in the right way.
5. Use the Opacity tool as shown to change the bevel's brightness, intensity, and visibility.
6. Move the two-dimensional lighting tool in the direction you want it to go to change the speed and direction of the light that is being applied to the effect.
7. In the rainbow color choice, click on a bevel color to choose it. The color that is currently chosen is shown in a row at the bottom of the color picker.
8. Press the OK button.

Apply Emboss layer style

1. Select a layer, and then choose Layer Styles from the drop-down menu.
2. Click on the Layer Styles tab in the Layer Properties box to open it.
3. In the group box that shows the effects you want to use, check the "Emboss" box. The new Emboss effect can be seen in the After pane, which has been updated. The "Preview on Image" box should be checked if you want to see how the changes will look on the real image.

4. Use the Size tool to change how far away the data's farthest edge is from the edge of the embossing. You can drag the tool to do this.
5. With the Opacity tool, you can change how bright, intense, and clear the embossing is.
6. Move the two-dimensional lighting tool in the direction you want it to go to change the speed and direction of the light that is being applied to the effect.
7. Click the "OK" button.

Apply Inner Glow layer styles

1. Select a layer, and then from the menu that shows, select Layer Styles.
2. Click on the Layer Styles tab in the Layer Properties box to open it.
3. Check the box next to "Inner Glow" in the group box that shows the results.
4. To select the depth of the layer data that the light can reach, move the Size slider to the right.
5. Move the Opacity tool to the left to change how bright the glow is. This will help you see the glow better.
6. Click on a bright color in the rainbow color picker to choose it. The color that is currently chosen is shown in a row at the bottom of the color picker.
7. Press the OK button.

Apply Drop Shadow layer styles

1. Select a layer, and then from the menu that shows, select Layer Styles.
2. Click on the Layer Styles tab in the Layer Properties box to open it.
3. In the group box that shows the effects, check the box next to "**Drop Shadow**." Then, hit "**OK**." Take note: The Drop Shadow effect might make You need to make the canvas bigger to see the whole effect if the data goes beyond what can be seen on the picture canvas, especially if the layer is the same size as the Background layer. This is especially true for layers that are the same size as the Background layer.
4. To change the distance between the layer data and the shadow, move the Size tool to the right. When the thing gets bigger, the shadow will become less clear.
5. Use the "**Opacity**" tool to change how bright the light is and how clear the shadow is.
6. Move the two-dimensional lighting tool in the direction you want it to go to change the speed and direction of the light that is being applied to the effect.
7. In the rainbow color choice, click on a shadow color to choose it. The color that is currently chosen is shown in a row at the bottom of the color picker.
8. Click the "OK" button.

Modify the visibility of the layer data

1. Pick out a layer that already has effects on it, and then click the Layer Styles button. Take note that if you change how visible layer data is, you will not change how visible any effects are that have been added to the layer.
2. Click on the Layer Styles tab in the Layer Properties box to open it.
3. In the group box that shows the effects you've selected, select the "Layer" checkbox. By

moving the Opacity tool, you can change how much light the layer data gives off and how clear it is.

4. Take the tick out of the Layers box to hide layer data.
5. Press the "**OK**" button.

Hide or display layer effects

1. The first step is to click on a layer in the Layers panel that already has effects on it.
2. Click the Layer Effects Visibility Toggle button to show or hide the effects. In the Layers panel, you can find this choice.
3. If an effect is on a layer, that layer gets an icon that looks like the effect. The icon can no longer be seen when the effect is hidden.

Copying and pasting layer styles

1. In the Layers panel, right-click on the layer that has the style you want to copy. A menu will open, and you can choose "Copy Layer Styles."
2. Right-click on the layer you want to style in the Layers box, and then select Paste Layer Styles from the menu that appears.

CHAPTER 11
MASKS

Masks are grayscale raster layers that cover parts of the layers in your picture. Depending on how the mask was made, it can cover the whole layer or only some of it. Masks can be used to make smooth changes between layers and to add special effects with accurate effects. You can use a mask to hide the parts of a picture that aren't directly related to the main subject, or you can use one to make a website's menu bar fade out over time. 256 different shades of gray are shown by mask pixels, and each shade shows a different amount of transparency. Pixels that are white show the underlying layers, pixels that are black hide the underlying layers, and pixels that are gray show different amounts of the underlying layers. The bottom layer in a picture or a layer group can't be a mask layer. If the mask layer is on the main level instead of inside a layer group, it will cover all levels below it. As long as the mask layer is part of the layer group, its effect will only be seen on the layers that are lower in the stacking order.

Display Masks

A mask overlay is shown over protected zones, which makes it easy to tell the difference between areas that are covered and areas that are not. To cover the face, there is a red sheet that can be seen through. When you change the amount of transparency of a mask in certain areas, the mask layer shows different amounts of red in those areas. Changing in an appropriate way. Any changes made to the mask are shown on the mask layer, whether you paint on it or change it in some other way. When you are changing a picture, you can choose to show or hide a mask layer.

Hiding or displaying Mask overlays and how to achieve it

In the Layers panel, there is a button in the upper right corner that says "Highlight mask area." The button will look like it's marked when the overlay is shown. You can choose to show or hide the mask overlay by going to the menu and choosing Layers, then View Overlay.

Adjust the level of transparency and color of the mask overlay

1. Right-click on the mask layer in the Layers box and select Properties from the menu that comes up.
2. From the menu, choose the Overlay tab.
3. Choose a color for the overlay by clicking the color area and then choosing it.
4. Use the tool that says "**Opacity**" to change how transparent something is.
5. Press the "**OK**" button.

Show or conceal a mask

1. Click the **Visibility Toggle** button in the Layers panel.
2. A button that lets the user know when the mask is on or off

3. A button that lets the user know when the mask is hidden

Create Masks

If you bring the picture file from your disk into the right program, you can use it to make a cover. When you use a picture as a mask for another picture, PaintShop Pro turns that picture into a grayscale copy of itself. There have been no changes made to the original picture. You could also make your own mask by changing one of the model masks that come with PaintShop Pro. A selection can be turned into a mask, which can either show or hide the selection. You can use this mask to get creative by starting with it and making other art effects. A mask can also be made from a channel by first splitting a picture which can be RGB, HSL, or CMYK. You can make a mask in this other way. PaintShop Pro turns each channel of a picture into a grayscale form of itself. If you use one of these channel photos as a guide, you can make a mask for either the original picture or a different one.

Create mask layers

1. Select the layer that you want to hide in the Layers panel.
2. Pick up the Layers menu and pick the New Mask Layer.

Select one of these choices after that:

- **Show All** shows all of the image's pixels below the surface.
- **Hide All** covers up all the pixels below

You can further:

- **Show the mask on the picture:** Pick out the Highlight mask area button in the layer's menu.
- Look at the picture the way it will be shown in print or online, without the mask layer or the transparency grid: Click View, then Palettes, then Overview.
- **Change the order of the layers that the mask is applied to**: To change where the mask layer is stacked in the Layers box, drag it to a different spot. The mask layer will be applied to all levels below the main level as soon as you drag it from the layer group to it.

Note: Print on the picture to see parts of the layer below.

Make masks out of the images you have

1. Open the picture you want to use as a mask.
2. Pick out the layer you want to hide in the Layers panel and click the "OK" button.
3. Go to the Layers menu and select **New Mask Layer > From Image**. This will bring up the Add Mask from the Image box.
4. Select the picture from the drop-down menu in the Source Window.
5. **Make your decision in the Create Mask From group box and pick one of the options below:**
   - **Source luminance:** The amount of masking the image gets is based on the luminance value of each pixel color. Masking has less of an effect on lighter colors and more of an effect on darker colors. Parts that are clear cover up the whole layer.

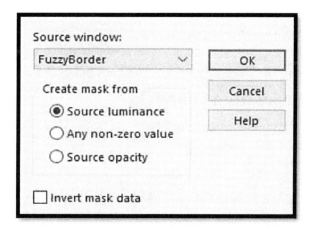

- **Any non-zero value:** Any number other than zero will mask, but there will be no gradation. It is white for pixels whose opacity value is between 1 and 255, and it is black for pixels that are not see-through. Parts that are clear cover up the whole layer.
- **Source opacity:** This value, which is based on how opaque the picture is, sets the amount of masking that is used. Pixels that are completely opaque don't mask anything, pixels that are partially transparent mask more, and pixels that are

completely transparent mask everything. When the "Invert mask data" box is checked, the mask's transparency will go the other way.

6. Click the "**OK**" button.

The chosen layer and the blank layer are added to a new layer group that was made. Your mask layer will only be applied to the layer that you have chosen at the moment. Select the image from the Layers window, and then click the Highlight mask area button to view the mask that has been applied to it. If you drag the mask layer from the layer group to the main level on the Levels menu, it will be applied to all the layers below it.

Create masks from selections

1. Select a layer in the document using the Selection tool, the Freehand Selection tool, or the Magic Wand tool.
2. **One of the things below must be done:**
   - To make a mask and hide the selection, go to the Layers menu and choose New Mask Layer > Hide Selection. To make a mask of everything but the selection, go to the Layers menu and choose New Mask Layer > Show Selection.

You can also:

- **Show the mask on the image:** Use the Highlight mask area button in the Layers panel to draw attention to a certain part of the mask.
- **Apply the mask layer to all of the layers that are below it:** The lines in the Layers panel can be used to move the mask layer from the layer group to the main level.

When you add a mask layer to the background, the background layer changes right away into a raster layer. The chosen layer and the blank layer are added to a new layer group that was made. Your mask layer will only be applied to the layer that you have chosen at the moment.

Generate masks from channels

1. Select **Split Channel** from the **Image** menu. Select one of these choices after that:
   - Split to HSL
   - Split to RGB
   - Split to CMYK
2. Pick the grayscale image that will be the basis for the mask you'll make.
3. Go to the Layers menu and select **New Mask Layer > From Image**. This will bring up the Add Mask from the Image box.
4. In the Source Window, use the drop-down menu to choose the channel you want to use for the cover.
5. In the dialog box, choose the Source luminance choice from the Create Mask From group. If you want the mask data's transparency to be inverted, select the "Invert mask data" box.
6. Click the "OK" button. The chosen layer and the blank layer are added to a new layer

group that was made. Your mask layer will only be applied to the layer that you have chosen at the moment.

Delete Masks

When working with masks, you can either erase them completely from a picture or join them with the layer below them and then delete the mask layer. You will not be able to change the mask directly from the layer below it after combining them.

1. Right-click on the mask layer in the Layers box and choose "Delete" from the menu that comes up. You will see a message asking if you want to merge the mask with the layer behind it.
2. Choose one of the routes below:
   - If you pick "Yes," the layers will be put together and the mask layer will be taken away.
   - Choosing "No" will get rid of the mask layer without changing the layer below it.

Edit Masks

To change a mask, you can either change the area it covers or the amount of hiding it gives. For example, painting over something to hide it will change the area, and using a gradient fill will change how much the object is hidden. A mask's transparency can be turned around so that black pixels turn white, white pixels turn black, and shades of gray turn into their mirror value, which is 255 minus the new value. With the help of a color, pattern, or texture mask, you can make effects that stand out. A gradient mask lets you change the opacity of an image by slowly fading it into or out of view. The opacity of an image can go from fully opaque to fully clear. A pattern or texture mask makes a design that repeats across an image and can be used to change the opacity of a picture.

Invert masks

1. In the Layers box, find a mask layer and click on its name.
2. Click on the Layers menu and pick the Invert Mask/Adjustment pick.

Develop a mask using a texture, pattern, or gradient

1. Make a fresh mask.
2. In the Layers box, click the Highlight mask area button to bring up the mask overlay.
3. Pick out the Flood Fill tool from the "Tools" bar and click on it. If you set the Match mode to None in the Tool Options box, you can fill all the pixels in the mask. This will give you a full picture.
4. Use the Materials box to pick a gradient, texture, or pattern.
5. To use the material for the center, click on the mask. To use the material for the background, right-click on the mask.

Load Masks

A mask from an alpha channel can be loaded into any picture, not just the one it was saved in. This is possible if you save a mask to an alpha channel in a PspImage file. Masks are examples of masks that can be added to pictures. You can find them in the PaintShop Pro application folder. There are gradients and different kinds of circles and squares in these sample masks that frame pictures. The extension for mask files is.PspMask.

Load Masks from the alpha channels

1. Pick out the layer you want to hide in the Layers panel.
2. Select Load/Save Mask from the Layers menu. The Load Mask from the Alpha Channel window box will appear when you choose it from the drop-down menu.
3. In the Load from Document drop-down box, choose the picture you want to use in the alpha channel. The alpha channel needs to be in this picture. Open photos that already have alpha channels should be the only ones that stay chosen.
4. The mask is in the alpha channel that you choose from the drop-down menu that is found below the document name.
5. Select one of the following choices from the Orientation group box to make your choice:
   - Fit to layer
   - As is
   - Fit to canvas
6. In the Options group box, pick one of the options below:
   - You can hide all masks to hide the pixels around a loaded mask that is smaller than the current image canvas or show all masks to show the pixels around a loaded mask that is smaller than the current image canvas.
   - Check the box next to "Invert transparency" to turn the mask image's transparency around.
7. Click on Load. The chosen layer and the blank layer are added to a new layer group that was made. Your mask layer will only be applied to the layer that you have chosen at the moment. The mask layer will be applied to all levels below the main level as soon as you drag it from the layer group to it.

Load masks from the disk

1. The first step is to click on the layer you want to hide in the Layers panel.
2. Select Load/Save Masks from the Layers menu. The Load Mask from Disk text box will appear when you choose Load Mask from Disk.
3. Click the drop-down menu inside the Mask group box to pick a mask or picture file to use. This is the face that was picked by the Preview group box on the photo canvas.
4. Select one of the following choices from the Orientation group box:
   - Changes the mask to fit the canvas that is currently showing the picture by expanding or shrinking it to fit.
   - In Fit to Layer, the mask is changed to fit the data of the active layer. This is done by

stretching or shrinking the mask as needed. If the layer hasn't been pushed past the edges of the canvas, this choice has the same effects as the Fit to Canvas option. Fit to Canvas is what it's set to by default.

- If you leave it as is, the mask will be in the upper left part of the running layer. The size of the mask doesn't change at all when this choice is chosen. If the mask image is smaller than the active layer, PaintShop Pro will hide any pixels that are outside the range of the mask image.

5. In PaintShop Pro, choose an option from the Options group box to set whether pixels around the loaded mask data are shown or hidden. One of the choices can be clicked on to do this. If the orientation is set to "As Is" and the loaded mask is smaller than the current picture frame, these settings will only change the mask in that case.

- The "Invert transparency" button can be used to flip the mask's transparency.
- Hide all masks and turn the pixels around the ones below into black ones that hide them.
- Display all masks that turn the pixels around them white, showing the pixels below.
- The image value changes the pixels around the mask to either white or black, based on whether the Show All Mask or Hide All Mask option was used. This choice can be used with both the Show All Mask and Hide All Mask choices.

6. Click on Load. When PaintShop Pro makes a new layer group, it adds the chosen layer and the mask layer to it. Your mask layer will only be applied to the layer that you have chosen at the moment. The mask layer will be applied to all levels below the main level as soon as you drag it from the layer group to it.

Save masks

There are separate files called PspMask that are used to store masks in PaintShop Pro. You can add a mask to another picture without first removing the face needed to open the source picture. The PspImage format will keep the mask along with the picture once it has been loaded. If you want to use the mask in a different picture or give it to someone else, you can save it to your hard drive or an alpha channel. An alpha channel is a place inside a picture where data can be stored. The alpha channel does not change the way a picture looks when masks or choices are saved there. You can save a mask to the alpha channel of either the picture that is currently selected or a different image. Take note that if you save the picture in a format other than PspImage, the alpha channels will be lost. You should always use the PspImage file when saving a master copy of your picture so that the alpha channels stay the same.

Save mask to disk

1. Go to the Layers menu and click on the mask layer.
2. Click on Layers, then Load/Save Mask, and finally Layers. Click on Save Mask to Disk to open the Save Mask to Disk box. People who store their masks in the usual Masks folder can see the names of their files in the Mask Files group box. In the New Mask group box, you can see the mask that is currently being used.
3. Click on the "Save" button.

...DocumentsCorel PaintShop Pro 2023 Masks is where mask files are stored by default in the program.

Save a mask to an alpha channel

1. Go to the Layers menu and click on the mask layer.
2. Select Load/Save Mask from the Layers menu. The Save Mask to Alpha Channel box will appear when you press the Save Mask to Alpha Channel button.
3. Choose an alpha channel from the "Add to Document" drop-down menu.

If you wish to save a mask to the alpha channel of another picture, you will first need to open the other image in PaintShop Pro and then click the alpha channel to activate it. Enter the new name that you would want to give the alpha channel into the box labeled "Name" if you want to alter its name.

4. Select the Save option.

CHAPTER 12
EFFECTS

You can add many different types of special effects to your photos with PaintShop Pro. These include 3D effects, artistic effects, lighting effects, reflection effects, and photographic effects. You can also paint with photos, stretch parts of images, or add frames to your photos to make them look different.

Choose Effects

From the Instant Effects panel, the Effect Browser, or the Effects submenu, you can choose which effects to use. Most of the effects can be made to fit your needs by changing the settings in the corresponding dialog boxes.

The dialogue windows for applying effects share similar aspects, including the following:

- The Before pane shows the picture as it was originally, and the After pane shows a sample of the picture with the current choices applied.
- When you click on the Load Preset drop-down menu, the most recently used preset will be chosen immediately. When you use presets, you can give different pictures the same settings.

Use the Instant Effects palette

You can quickly add effects that have already been set up by using the Instant Effects menu. You can use this simple way to make an effect when you don't want to fool around with the controls. If you use one of the effects dialog boxes to make a preset, it will show up in the Instant Effects palette under the name User Defined as soon as it's done. The Strength, Color Match, and Smooth Image settings are all in the AI Style Transfer category. These settings let you change the result.

Use Effect Browser

This is where you can see how different effects will look on your picture before you actually use them. You can see any presets you make in the Effect Browser, along with the presets that come with PaintShop Pro and any others that you make. Any other presets you have saved to the picture are used along with the effect's basic preset when PaintShop Pro makes the thumbnail previews that you see in the Effect Browser. The setting is kept in a file type called PspScript that can be opened in PaintShop Pro.

Select effects from the Effects menu

1. Use the "Effects" menu to choose an effect group and a specific effect to use. Pick "Effects," then "Distortion Effects," and finally "Twirl."

2. Either type in the right settings by hand or use the Load Preset drop-down box to select a configuration that you have already saved. In the window called "After," you can see a preview of the result. Keep in mind that not all effects can be used with settings.
3. Click the "OK" button.

You can also:

- **Save settings for reuse:** To save a preset, click the Save Preset button, type a name into the "Preset name" box, and then click the OK button.
- **Reset settings to default values:** From the drop-down menu next to Load Preset, choose Default.
- **Restriction of an impact on a certain area**: first make a choice, and then choose the result you want.

Choose effects from the Instant Effects palette

1. In the Instant Effects palette, use the drop-down menu right below the preview at the very top of the palette to choose a group to work with. To see the Instant Effects palette, go to View > Palettes > Instant Effects if you can't see it already.
2. When you click on a thumbnail, the effect that goes with it will be added to the preview in the palette.
3. If you double-click on a thumbnail, the effect will be applied to all of the photos you have chosen as well as the live image. Except for the AI-powered effect, effects build on top of each other. Every time you double-click; a new effect is added to the list of effects that have already been caused.

The effect can be undone by clicking the "Undo" button (in the Adjust and Edit tabs). Images saved in the RAW format are turned into JPEG files when you add effects to them in the Effects panel on the Manage tab. You can find your customized presets in the User Defined area of the Instant Effects palette the next time you run the program. You can save these settings in any of the effect dialog boxes.

Make your selections using the Effect Browser

1. Go to the menu and choose Effects > Effect Browser.
2. **From the tree structure in the left pane, pick one of the following options:**
   - Click the Presets box to see a sneak peek of all the effects that have been used on the picture.
   - Go to the Effects folder and click on a subdirectory, like 3D Effects, Artistic Effects, or Photo Effects, to see a preview of a group of effects. PaintShop Pro will look through the chosen folder and make thumbnails of the pictures. Each thumbnail will have the effects that were used on the original picture.

3. **To choose an effect setting, click on a small picture of the effect.**
4. Click the "Apply" button. You can also:
   - **Adjust the currently chosen default setting:** Click the Modify button and then make changes in the text box that comes up to change how the effect works. Please keep in mind that this button is disabled for effects that can't be changed.
   - **Adjust the size of the preview thumbnail:** When you go to File > Preferences > General Program Preferences from the menu bar, a window will pop up. Click the Display and Caching link on the left side of that window. Set a number for the Size (Pixels) control that is in the group box with the Effect browser thumbnails.
   - **Limit an effect to a certain area:** Choose something, then choose the result you want.

Both the preset that is set as the default and any settings that you have saved before are shown in the thumbnail previews for each effect in the Effect Browser. The main folder of the program has a folder called "Presets" that holds the presets. The script files that hold presets are called.PspScript files are kept in the main program folder. You can change where the setup files are kept.

Apply 3D Effects

When you use the 3D effects, you can make pictures or choices that look like they are in three dimensions. These effects are great for adding to pictures that are used on websites.

Buttonize

The Buttonize effect can be used on any selection, layer, or squashed picture to make it look like it has square inset or rectangular buttons. This effect gives the picture or pick a three-dimensional edge that makes it look like it is raised. Take the drop-down menu in the top menu bar and choose Effects > 3D Effects > Buttonize. This will bring up the Buttonize dialog box.
Controls for the following things may be found in the Buttonize dialog box:
- **Height:** This number, given in pixels, tells you how tall the button is.
- **Width** The width of the button is shown by this number, which is given in pixels.
- **Opacity:** This gives the button a smooth look by giving its edges a soft shading.
- **Transparent:** This gives the sides of the button a solid color, which makes them sharp and easy to see.
- **Solid:** This gives the sides of the button a rounded look by covering them with a solid color. First, choose a solid color, then use the Buttonize command from the drop-down menu to make a button with a colored edge.
- **Color:** There is a color option that lets you choose a border color for the button. One way to choose a color is to right-click the color box and chooses "Recent Colors." The other way is to click on the color box and choose "Color." You can choose either of these two choices.

Chisel

By adding a border that looks like it's three-dimensional, the Chisel effect makes it look like a pick or layer has been carved out of stone. You can make the carved area see-through, so the colors below the surface can be seen, or you can make it the same color as the background. Take the drop-down menu in the Effects menu and choose Chisel from the 3D Effects menu. This will bring up the Chisel dialog box.

Controls for the following things can be found in the Chisel dialog box:

- **Size:** This choice sets the overall pixel size of the carved area.
- **Transparent:** You can see the colors below through the cutout area.
- **Solid color:** The carved area has the same color all over.
- **Color** lets you pick a different color for the background of the carved area. You can use the Color dialog box if you click on the color box. You can use the Recent Colors dialog box if you right-click on the color box.

Cutout

The Cutout effect makes it look like a part of the image has been cropped out, which lets the user see through the picture and down to a lower level. There is a part of the picture you can choose to work with before adding this effect, but it is not required. From the Effects menu, choose Effects > 3D Effects > Cutout from the drop-down menu. This will bring up the Cover dialog box.

Controls for the following things may be found in the Cutout dialog box:

- **Vertical** tells us where the inside and outside will be in relation to the vertical plane. If you change the setting, you can move the interior to the bottom of the picture or the top of the picture.
- **Horizontal:** Sets the interior's direction and draws the bottom line of the horizontal plane. You can change the setting to move the inside to the left or right.
- **"Opacity"** lets you change how opaque the shadow is, and
- **"Blur"** lets you change how blurry the shadow is. As you raise the blur level, the shadow gets less defined along its sides and becomes more spread out.
- **Shadow color** lets you pick a shade of color for the shadow. If you click on the color box, you can bring up the Color dialog box. If you right-click on the color box, you can bring up the Recent Colors dialog box, instead. You can choose either of these two choices.
- **Fill the interior with color:** This option lets you fill the inside with the most recent color choice. You can click on the color box to open the Color dialog box and pick a new color. You can also right-click on the color box to open the Recent Colors dialog box. Each of these has choices available to you. If you don't check this box, the picture will be filled in over the gap.

The Drop Shadow

With Drop Shadow, a shadow is added to the background of the current selection. The most popular way to use it is to give the text a three-dimensional look. Before you can add a drop shadow to the whole picture, you need to make sure there is enough empty space around it. Take a look at the Image menu and pick either the Add Borders or Canvas Size command to do this. To get to the Drop Shadow text box, go to the Effects menu, pick 3D Effects, and then pick Drop Shadow.

Controls for the following things can be found in the Drop Shadow dialog box:

- Vertical, which sets the height at which the shadow goes? You can also change the height by changing the crosshair at the end of the line that shows the offset, which is on the left side of the dialog box.
- Horizontal, the width of the shadow is set by its horizontal position. The width can also be changed by moving the crosshair at the end of the line that shows the offset, which is on the left side of the text box.
- Opacity is what makes the shadow opaque. When this value is lowered, the drop shadow is less obvious.
- The blur factor decides how fuzzy the shadow will be.
- When you click on Color, you can pick the color for the drop shadow. One way to choose a color is to right-click the color box and chooses "Recent Colors." The other way is to click on the color box and choose "Color." You can choose either of these two choices.
- When you click on Shadow on a New Layer, the drop shadow is put on a separate raster layer.

If you choose the Border with drop shadow script from the Script drop-list on the Script menu, you can get an effect that looks like Drop Shadow. The image you get from this will be like the Drop Shadow effect.

Inner Bevel

There is an effect called "Inner Bevel" that can make the edges of a pick or an item that is surrounded by transparency look like they are three-dimensional. The thing is the same size as before this effect. The Inner Bevel effect settings can be set by hand, you can choose one of the preset effects that come with the app, or you can start with a preset effect and then change its parameters. It is possible to use the Inner Bevel command on an image that has a clear background, a colored background with a selection, or a colored background and a layer. If a layer doesn't have a pick or a clear area, the effect will be applied to the edges of the layer instead. You can use the Eraser Tool, promote a selection, or copy and paste a selection as a new layer to make a layer with transparency. One of the other choices is to move a selection to a higher layer. From the menu, you can also choose Effects > 3D Effects > Inner Bevel to open the text box for The Inner Bevel effect.

The following controls can be found in the dialog box titled "Inner Bevel:"

- **Bevel** talks about the shape of the bevel.
- **Width** is a necessary field that shows the width in pixels.
- **Smoothness** controls the angle of the slope (how sharp it is) and the edge's thickness. As this number goes up in the range, the corners will become less sharp. As it goes down, the edges will look narrower and sharper.
- **Depth** tells you how high the edge is and lets you control it. The edge will be easier to see as the number of this parameter goes up.
- It's the atmosphere that changes the brightness of the whole picture.
- How shiny something is affects how it looks when it reflects light. If you raise the value, the picture will look glossier and the highlights will stand out more. The highlights get less noticeable as the value goes down.
- **Hue**: In the hue property, you can change the color of the light that's shining on the picture. You can either click on a color in the picture or right-click on the color box to open the Recent Colors dialog box. Also, clicking on the color box will open the Color dialog box. If you do any of these things, the light will change color.
- **Angle**: It is the angle that changes which lines look bright and which look dark. If you measure the position of the needle in degrees around the circle, you can see which way the light source is coming from. You can type in a number, click on the circle, drag the needle, or set a number by hand in the control to change the amount.
- **Intensity**: You can change the intensity of the light coming from a certain direction. You should remember that the Ambience parameter sets the general brightness of the picture before the Intensity parameter is used.
- **Elevation** shows the angle above the picture that the light source is at. When the angle is set to 90 degrees, the light source is right above. The light source moves closer to the picture when the number is lowered. This makes the shadows longer.

Outer Bevel

The Outer Bevel effect makes a selection look like it has three dimensions by making the edges look like they are higher. It makes the choices bigger by the width of the bevel when you do this. You will need to make a pick somewhere in the picture before you can choose the Outer Bevel command from the Effects menu. Click on the Effects menu, pick 3D Effects, and then pick Outer Bevel from the drop-down menu. This will bring up the Outer Bevel effect dialog box.

The Outer Bevel dialog box includes the below controls:

- **Bevel:** It talks about the shape of the bevel.
- **Width:** This number, given in pixels, tells you how wide the curved edge is.
- **Smoothness:** The level of smoothness controls both the angle of the slope (how sharp it is) and the edge's thickness. As this number goes up in the range, the corners will become less sharp. As it goes down, the edges will look narrower and sharper.
- **Depth** tells you how high the edge is and lets you control it. The edge will be easier to see

as the number of this parameter goes up.

- Adjusting the brightness of the picture all over is done by the ambience.
- The amount of shine on the surface changes how reflective it looks. If you raise the value, the picture will look glossier and the highlights will stand out more. The highlights get less noticeable as the value goes down.
- **Hue:** The hue property tells the picture what color the light is that is shining on it. You can either click on a color in the picture or right-click on the color box to open the Recent Colors dialog box. Also, clicking on the color box will open the Color dialog box. If you do any of these things, the light will change color.
- **Angle:** Which sides look bright and which look dark depends on the angle. If you measure the position of the needle in degrees around the circle, you can see which way the light source is coming from. You can type in a number, click on the circle, drag the needle, or set a number by hand in the control to change the amount.
- **Intensity**: With intensity, you can change how bright the light is coming from a certain direction. You should remember that the Ambience parameter sets the general brightness of the picture before the Intensity parameter is used.
- **Elevation** shows the angle of slope of the light source in relation to the picture. When the angle is set to 90 degrees, the light source is right above. The light source moves closer to the picture when the number is lowered. This makes the shadows longer.

Adding Text to Images

1. Select the Text tool from the Tools toolbar.

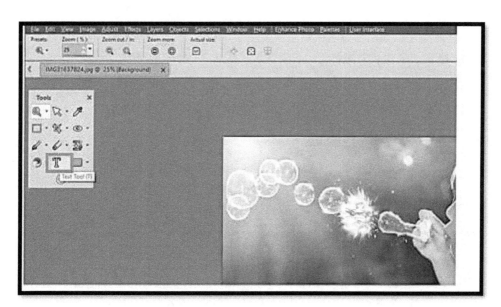

2. Customize text settings such as font, size, style, color, and stroke on the Tool Options palette.

139

- **Note:** Choose between Points (for print) and Pixels (for web) in the Units drop-down menu.

3. Choose a text type from the Create As drop-down menu:

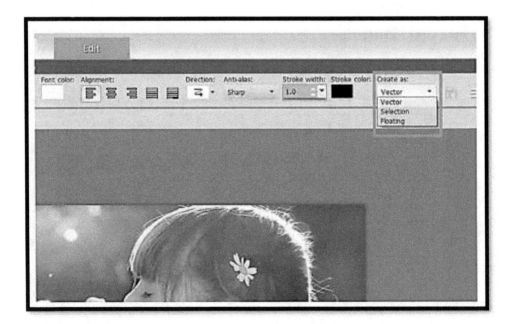

- **Vector:** Editable text on a vector layer (default).
- **Selection:** Text creates a selection marquee filled with the layer underneath.
- **Floating:** Raster text as a floating selection (not editable).

4. Click where you want the text, type, and hit Apply on the Tool Options palette.
   - A bounding box appears around the text.

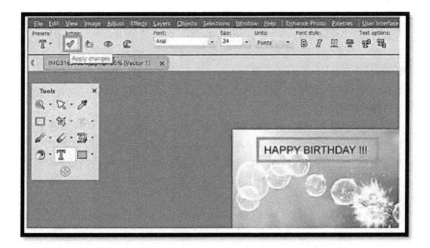

5. **Adjust text position:**
   - Move: Place the pointer in the center of the bounding box, and drag it to the desired location.
   - Rotate: Position the pointer over a corner until it becomes a two-way arrow, then drag it up or down to rotate.

Applying Text Effects and Styles

1. **Add Text:**
   - Open Corel PaintShop Pro and create a new project or open an existing one.
   - Select the Text tool from the toolbar. It's represented by the "A" icon.
   - Click on the canvas where you want to add text and start typing. You can adjust the font, size, and color of the text in the options toolbar at the top.

2. **Access Text Styles:**
   - Once you've added your text, you can apply predefined text styles or create custom effects.
   - In the Layers palette, locate the text layer you want to apply the style to.
   - Right-click on the text layer and select "Edit Text" to access the Text Tool Options dialog box.

3. **Apply Predefined Styles:**
   - In the Text Tool Options dialog box, click on the "Styles" tab.
   - Here, you'll find a variety of predefined text styles categorized under different themes like Basic, Decorative, Grunge, etc.
   - Select the desired text style by clicking on it. The style will be applied to your text immediately.

4. **Customize Text Effects:**
   - If you want to customize the text effects further, you can do so by adjusting various parameters.
   - In the Text Tool Options dialog box, go to the "Text" tab.

- Here, you can modify parameters such as font, size, color, alignment, spacing, and more to create custom text effects.
- Experiment with different settings until you achieve the desired look for your text.

5. **Layer Effects**:
- You can also apply layer effects to your text layer to add additional visual enhancements.
- In the Layers palette, right-click on the text layer and select "Layer Properties."
- In the Layer Properties dialog box, go to the "Effects" tab.
- Here, you can apply various effects such as drop shadow, outer glow, bevel, and emboss to your text layer to give it a more polished appearance.

6. **Save and Export**:
- Once you're satisfied with the text effects and styles applied, remember to save your project.
- You can then export your design to various formats for sharing or printing.

Apply art media effects

Adding effects from the Art Media area to a picture can make it look like it was painted or sketched. You can also use charcoal, chalk, and pencil to make an effect that looks like it was made with traditional art supplies.

Black Pencil Brush Strokes

While the Black Pencil effect is similar to the Charcoal effect, it uses finer brushstrokes to make a picture with more detail. To open the Black Pencil dialog box, go to the Effects menu and select Art Media Effects. Then, select Black Pencil from the drop-down menu.

Controls for the following things can be found in the Black Pencil dialog box:

- What determines the number of blows and how hard they are is up to **Detail**.
- **Opacity** is the tool that lets you choose how strong the effect is. For each rise in the value, the picture will show more of the effect and less of its original look.

Brush Strokes

The Brush Strokes effect makes it look like the picture you're working on is an oil or watercolor drawing. To get to the Brush Strokes dialog box, go to the Effects menu and choose Art Media Effects > Brush Strokes from the drop-down menu.

The following editable options can be found inside the Brush Stroke dialog box:

- **Softness** determines how blurry the picture is
- **Bristles** tell the program how many bristles to use when making the brush
- With **width**, you can change how wide the brush is.

- **"Opacity"** controls how strong the effect is, and "length" sets how long the brushstrokes are.
- **Density**: The number of strokes in the picture is set by the density.
- The **angle** tells the program which sides to show and which to hide. If you measure the position of the needle in degrees around the circle, you can see which way the light source is coming from. You can type in a number, click on the circle, drag the needle, or set a number by hand in the control to change the amount.
- **Color** lets you pick a color for the light that's shining along the shapes of the structures. You can use the Color dialog box if you click on the color box. You can use the Recent Colors dialog box if you right-click on the color box.

Charcoal

The Charcoal effect is like the Black Pencil effect, but the picture has less clarity because the strokes are thicker. From the drop-down menu, choose Effects > Art Media Effects > Charcoal to open the Charcoal dialog box.

The following controls can be found inside the dialog box for the Charcoal effect:

- What determines the number of blows and how hard they are is up to **Detail**.
- **Opacity** is the tool that lets you choose how strong the effect is. As the Opacity number goes up, the picture shows more of the effect and less of its original look.

Colored Chalk

Using the colors that are already in the picture, the Colored Chalk effect makes it look like the picture was drawn with colored chalk. The strokes are much bigger when this effect is used than when the Colored Pencil effect is used. To get to the Colored Chalk dialog box, go to the Effects menu and choose Art Media Effects > Colored Chalk from the drop-down menu.

In the Colored Chalk dialog box, you can find controls for the following:

- **Detail** controls how many lines you make and how strong they are.
- The setting that tells you how strong the effect is is **opacity**. As the Opacity number goes up, the picture shows more of the effect and less of its original look.

It is possible to make an effect that looks like colored chalk by using the Chalk tool, which is on the Tools panel.

Colored Pencil

With the Colored Pencil effect, the colors in the picture are used to make it look like the subject was drawn with colored pencils. The only difference between this effect and the Colored Chalk effect is that the lines are much thinner. Click on Effects in the drop-down menu, then click on Art Media Effects, and finally click on Colored Pencil to open the window.

Controls for the following options can be found in the Colored Pencil dialog box:

- **Detail** controls how many strokes are used and how strong they are.
- **Opacity** is the tool that lets you choose how strong the effect is. As the Opacity number goes up, the picture shows more of the effect and less of its original look.

Pencil

The Pencil effect makes the edges of the picture stand out more and changes their color, making it look like a pencil sketch instead of a photo. In the Effects menu, go to the drop-down menu and choose Pencil from the list of effects. This will bring up the Pencil dialog box.

Controls for the following options can be found in the Pencil dialog box:

- **Luminance** lets you change the overall brightness of the picture.
- **Blur** is the effect that changes how fuzzy a picture is. There is less sharpness in the picture as the number goes up.
- **Color** lets you pick a color for the image's background, which is the part that doesn't have any edges around it. If you want to change a color in the picture, you can click on the color box to open the Color dialog box, or you can right-click on the color box to open the Recent Colors dialog box. If you do any of these things, the light will change color.
- **Intensity** tells you how different the background and edges of the picture are from each other. More and more details will be seen as the contrast is turned up.

Conclusion

In conclusion, Corel PaintShop Pro is an all-encompassing tool for graphic design and image editing. It provides a wide range of capabilities that are designed to cater to the requirements of those who are just starting out as well as those who are more experienced. PaintShop Pro has a user-friendly interface in addition to extensive capabilities, allowing users to quickly and easily manage and organize photographs, edit and enhance images with precision, and do all of these tasks. By providing users with a versatile toolkit, workspaces that can be customized, and navigation that is easy to understand, users are able to unleash their creativity and generate beautiful results. With Corel PaintShop Pro, you have the ability to bring your ideas to life in a way that is both simple and effective, regardless of whether you are retouching photographs, producing digital art, or designing graphics.

INDEX

D

H

I

N

Q

R

156

www.ingramcontent.com/pod-product-compliance
Lightning Source LLC
LaVergne TN
LVHW081527050326
832903LV00025B/1662